The All-American Industrial Motel

A Memoir

Doug Crandell

CHICAGO
REVIEW
PRESS

Library of Congress Cataloging-in-Publication Data
Crandell, Doug.
The all-American industrial motel : a memoir / Doug Crandell.
p. cm.
ISBN-13: 978-1-55652-616-9
ISBN-10: 1-55652-616-4
1. Crandell, Doug—Childhood and youth. 2. Crandell, Doug—Homes and haunts—Indiana—Wabash Region. 3. Authors, American—21st century—Biography. 4. Wabash Region (Ind.)—Social life and customs. 5. Indiana—Intellectual life. I. Title.
PS3603.R377Z46 2007
818'.603—dc22
[B]
2006019012

Cover and interior design: Sarah Olson
Cover illustration: Kathleen Judge

Copyright ©2007 by Doug Crandell
All rights reserved
First edition
Published by Chicago Review Press, Incorporated
814 North Franklin Street
Chicago, Illinois 60610
ISBN-10: 1-55652-616-4
ISBN-13: 978-1-55652-616-9
Printed in the United States of America
5 4 3 2 1

For my father,
who taught me that being a man
means having the courage to change.

It doesn't matter who my father was; it matters who I remember he was.
—ANNE SEXTON

The labor movement has always been the haven for the dispossessed,
the despised, the neglected, the downtrodden, the poor.
—ASA P. RANDOLPH

Contents

PART III: AUGUST 1990

INTRODUCTION

When I was a child, my mother would let me ride with her to deliver my father's dinner to the Celotex ceiling tile factory. They were in love then, or so it seemed. She would pack his chicken and dumplings in a warm Crock-Pot, slip on a pair of heels, and spray her neck with hyacinth perfume. At the factory, I would marvel at how big the men were, their shirtsleeves twitching with every bend of their strong arms. I'd watch my father as he snuffed a cigarette out into the cuff of his jeans, the smoke puffing around the ankle of his battered work boots. Why he would do that, or flick his ashes into that cuff, or put a cigarette out against a wooden slat or a stone in the field and then place the smashed butt in the cuff, I had no idea, but I longed to find out, to become a man like him, do his work and wear his clothes. I wanted to smoke like him, hold my own ashes near my foot, carry them around like little dusty mysteries, and dump them when I saw fit, perhaps at a lunch break or walking alone in the pasture.

While my mother and father talked about the farm, I'd breathe in the smell of Salem Lights and sit on the knee of an enormous mute named Garner. His hands were heavy and sandpapery, as hot as the factory air, and he'd cradle my tiny hand in his, fiddling with the small nails, his massive thigh like a tree trunk under my butt. At the factory, to hold another man's son imparted a godfatherlike quality, whereas to put your own son on your lap showed weakness, a desire to soften a boy, make him unfit for the calloused world he would soon inhabit. Daddies didn't hold their boys, but Garner held me, and I relished every moment: his gentle, wordless examination of my cuticles, his approving smile in my father's direction, and his velvet pat on my rear as I crawled down.

By the time I came to work at the factory in the summer of 1990, Garner had been taken by the asbestos and whisked up into the sooty sky above the unregulated smokestacks. What I learned about being a man that summer was just as elusive, mostly wordless, and always contradictory.

PART I

June 1990

"What goes on between the father and son—and what does not go on between them—is surely the most important determinant of whether the boy will become a man."

—FRANK PITTMAN,
*Man Enough: Fathers, Sons, and
the Search for Masculinity*

DADDY'S LITTLE FURRY FRIEND

I t was the end of my first full day on the job. The time clock in the break room ticked midnight, making it June 5, 1990. A line of men stood fiddling with their punch cards, flicking them against dirty-legged Dickies, while others used them to fan themselves. One man named Ronald, whose wrinkled skin hung like soft leather from his face, used the corner of his time card to clean between his few teeth. I tried to act like I wasn't looking for my dad, but I turned slowly around in line to try and spot him. Carl, my dad's best friend, entered the break room, nodding at me, his short little body outfitted in work clothes fit for an adolescent. Someone asked him if the twins were going to swim all summer and he smiled and nodded. "Can't keep 'em out of that pool." He was proud of that fact, and that he'd been able to build them a place to cool off on his grain farm. Like my dad had done before we lost our farm, Carl worked both the factory and the farm, and paid heavily for it.

My father was nowhere to be found. I hadn't spent much time with him since my grandmother's funeral almost six months earlier. At the wake, I'd hoped to see him crying, broken down, needing a son to lift him up and provide some love, but he stood stoically by the casket, not a trace of emotion in his eyes. I'd hugged him and he stuffed a twenty-dollar bill into my shirt pocket. Since then I'd talked to him on the phone, but that was always just a formality, after I'd spoken with my mother about what I was eating or how the weather was at school in Muncie, just an hour away from them.

The time clock rattled with a metallic buzz, and one by one the third-shift men shoved their cards into the metal box bolted to the wall and carried themselves and their lunch boxes out the door to the parking lot. I could hear the engines of Impalas, Rams, and El Caminos revving up and peeling out the front gates as I waited alone on a bench in the break room for my dad. He was my ride home.

The motors on the greasy vending machines whirled as the time clock ticked fifteen after midnight. Finally, the rear door of the break room opened and my dad walked in. At first, I couldn't determine what was different. He didn't speak as he plunked a quarter into the coffee machine, and then waited for the paper cup to drop and fill with black. I stared at his head. He always wore a finely starched farmer's cap, usually one with a seed corn company name on it, on his bald head. Now, his cap looked fuller, more substantial. A thick crop of gray hair rested above his ears, and he had bangs. It was stiff and unnatural to be certain, but there it was, sticking out from his cap: a maladjusted toupee, shyly waiting for the right moment to be unveiled.

My dad gingerly escorted his steaming cup of coffee to the bench, careful not to spill a drop. He brought it to his lips and blew slightly over the rim. I ogled his new possession as he sat down, not looking at me. I took my eyes from his head momentarily to look at his burly hand cradling the cup. Nicks split the skin on his knuckles, and light brown spots pocked his broad fingers. My eyes soon strayed back to that head, to the poorly configured hairpiece that couldn't have shocked me more had it been alive, which, with its grayish bristles and mousy texture, it almost appeared to be—surely a member of the rodent family. I was about to say something about it, but, perhaps sensing it, he said, "You've got to keep your eye on the overtime roster, son." He slurped his coffee, making a sound like a zipper coming up. His steel-toed boots were laced as usual, the long brown cords strung through each eyelet and crisscrossed at the top from one gold clasp to the other, the extra length wrapped around the back. Mine, the same standard-issue boots from the factory's prisonlike supply room, were loosely tied and very new, not worn and beaten-up like his.

"If you don't sign up every day on the clipboard, Doug, you won't get the extra shifts. It's in the contract. The foreman can't call you if your name isn't on it. You've got to sign that sheet every day."

I felt like a failure. I still had one class to complete to graduate from Ball State University, and moving back home to take the factory job meant I hadn't made it on my own. But the union pay was good, and I had student loans to repay.

"Did you hear what I said?" My father looked at me, searching for any sign I'd understood. I nodded.

He took a braver drink of the coffee and brushed some filaments of rock wool from his pants. The stuff looked like slightly toasted cotton candy. It came out of 2,600-degree cupolas that heated a mixture of coke and limestone rock and spun it into fibers that were then rolled into gigantic heaps. The factory was covered with the stuff. It clung to everything, dangling in the nooks and crannies, hanging along the exposed pipes, and sticking between every concrete block and board slat. The fibers acted like nearly invisible filaments of glass, creating small pimples if brushed into bare skin, itching like poison ivy in the heat, and causing rashes and ill tempers. My father, who'd worked in the factory for twenty years by the time I started there, rarely carried rock wool on his pressed blue jeans, Carhartt jacket, or work shirts. He kept his clothes tidy.

The men working the next shift—from midnight until 8:00 A.M.—had been clocked in for more than half an hour when my dad finally stood up and adjusted his cap. The toupee seemed to be sewn to the cap itself, the whole thing moving as one piece.

"Come on," he said in a monotone, as if any change in inflection might cause Mr. Toupee to lose his footing and slip, along with the cap, off his head and onto the scuffed linoleum floor. I didn't ask where we were going as I trailed behind him. We plodded along the eerie factory floor, the metal machines lurking in a steaming haze.

The first shift carried a skeleton crew made up of men who either had been demoted to such an owl-like existence by lipping off to management, or simply preferred to work late-night hours. As I followed my dad, we passed men working on jobs named A-car and B-car, gel makeup, paper operator, paint booth man, and simple maintenance. Each of the workers briefly stopped and tipped their heads at my dad, and a couple of them gave him the thumbs-up. Their required safety glasses, the ones I wore like a dork, were absent.

Finally, after walking the factory floor for a block or so, my dad opened a door leading down a cold hallway. It was air-conditioned, unlike the rest of the boiling-hot factory. We made our way into a cramped office. Here the tile orders were processed and loaded onto the waiting semis that throttled like long, red-eyed behemoths in the darkness off the crumbling docks. My dad's counterpart, the man who was to perform his job from midnight until the sun rose over the glassy lagoon next to the rear of the factory, was nowhere in sight.

"Sit down," my dad instructed. The cool air made my body shiver; it had to be fifty degrees in the office. Later, I'd find out what a luxury the air conditioning was, like the privileges of an extended break or bidding on the best jobs. I sat down in a steel chair, its padded seat all but gone. I looked around and noticed something right away: there wasn't any rock wool clinging to anything inside the tiny office. It had been swept clean. The scent of pine cleanser hung in the cold air.

The ashtray on the desk was spotless, serving as a heavy glass paper-weight on top of a stack of transport bills. My dad switched on the desk lamp, opened the drawer at his knees, and pulled out two pencils sharpened to perfection. He inspected them nonetheless and handed me one. "Pull your chair over here," he said, a look of concentration on his face. For the next twenty minutes, he showed me a mock-up of the sheet used to get the coveted overtime. He used his big forefinger to direct my attention to the blank spaces where I was to write my name, and showed me which boxes to check to ensure the optimal conditions for being called in. It was a complex system that had been hammered out by the union and management a year earlier in the contract negotiations that blistered up every three years, causing the men in ties and the men in work clothes to angrily debate and fight for advantage. I tried to listen carefully, to grasp the nuances of how the system worked—its flaws and how to beat the odds to get the desirable overtime pay—but I was at a loss. He was about to ask me if I had any questions when the phone on the desk rang. My father's hand shot across the desk and he plucked the receiver from the cradle before it could ring again.

"Hi," he said into the phone. "Yes. Sounds good." His voice was intimate, yet more formal than when talking with my mother. I sat next to him, chilled to the bone. I'd only been living back at home for a week, and during that time the same kind of enigmatic calls arrived at the house. Sometimes, when my mother answered, whoever was on the other end hung up, leaving her staring at the receiver, the dial tone crackling, her eyes filled with hurt. Now, my dad hung up the phone with precision and began to fold the sheet we'd been studying into a neat square. It was approaching 1:00 A.M. He stood and handed me the cube of paper to me.

"You take the car home. I've got another eight to pull here." He seemed as fresh as if starting a new morning. "Why?" I asked. He smirked a little and patted me on the back as I stood. "Son, you better get it into your head now about grabbing these extra shifts when you can." With that, he opened the door to the office as if dismissing me from an interview.

I stood, not wanting to leave. Why had he gotten a toupee? Why couldn't we talk about my grandmother's death? I tucked the sheet I was to study into my back pocket and started to walk down the tiny hall. Through a small window I could see my father working at the desk, carefully preparing the paperwork that the trucker who sat idling in the dark outside needed. I stopped and stared in at my dad. That toupee. It signaled something. I sensed in him a brokenness, a hardship he could not find words for, or at least not words he was willing to use.

. . .

Between 1985 and 1989 my father lost both of his parents and a farm. He was forced to auction off the household items and farm implements his own father and mother had used all their lives. At a court hearing to determine his bankruptcy status, a county circuit court judge had him take the stand. At the end of the judge's questioning about income and various debtors, he had my father stand up. "Take out your wallet, Mr. Crandell," he said. My dad handed his wallet to the bailiff, who handed it to a clerk. She rummaged through it and passed it back through the chain to my father as if it were a bucket of water ushered along a fire brigade. The clerk took a piece of paper to the judge and handed it up to him. He read it while my father stood in the witness box. "Let the records show Mr. Crandell has seven dollars on his person." My father slowly put his wallet away and was ordered to leave the stand. Out in the courthouse lobby, other tired and foreclosed farmers sat in threadbare jackets, smelling of dried manure and diesel fuel. Many had already taken jobs at convenience stores or had broken out their musty suits from twenty years before to try and hawk insurance. My dad hadn't been able to depend on just farming to support his family for almost fifteen years by the time he took the stand; he had the factory job and he felt fortunate, but that also meant he'd be required to pay as many of his debts as possible, leaving just enough to get by.

. . .

I continued to spy on him through the window. He was back on the phone, smiling.

THOSE MASCULINE BURIED SECRETS

In 1981, when I was thirteen years old, some factory men helped my dad build me a basketball court. The sweaty workers smoothed the concrete with flat shovels, pushing the slick gray mixture into spots that were uneven. I watched their strong, dark arms, roped with oddly shaped muscles, pulse in the heat. When the men were around, their hairy bodies pushing and pulling and lifting, it never failed to make me feel inadequate. My own string-bean arms were blindingly pale, and I couldn't imagine having anything other than my hairless, concave chest or smooth, weak legs.

The summer sun baked us as the towering stalks of corn across from the court rustled their leaves like great, upright grasshoppers rubbing their legs together. The corn silk gave off the spicy, tangy smell of growth and made me think of my father's aftershave. The men had come to the farm as a favor to my father, who was revered for helping out his fellow union men and their families. He'd work extra shifts so a union buddy would have the money for a child who needed an important operation. He'd volunteer to work in place of a man who'd forgotten a special anniversary or birthday celebration so the guy could attend. He would even act as a lay therapist, listening to men's problems and giving them advice. But I wouldn't be privy to those stories about my dad for years. Now, as I followed the men scrambling to keep the cement from setting up, I knew only that my father and I had a secret, and it made me feel more like a man now that he had trusted me with his confidence. The thing we'd hidden, already buried under two tons of sand and a layer of flat steel bars, was being covered over with wet cement.

The last churning truck backed up to dump the final load of cement into the farthest corner of what would be a half-court playing surface. I was going to learn to be the next Kent Benson, an Indiana University basketball icon my father greatly admired. How I would manage to grow Benson's sideburns was something I hadn't figured out yet; my face was absent any beard except a few little hairs I sometimes confused with lint in the mirror of my bedroom.

The men worked close together and the heat was stifling; the scent of Ivory soap only slightly masked the body odor wafting around their saggy jeans. Ass cracks were visible everywhere, and I assumed part of being a man was to expose your flat butt some. But mine was round and ample, and my jeans were tight, not droopy. Carl, a short man with stubby legs, yanked and pulled on a long harness attached to a smoothing board, creating a gleaming finish to the final section of the court. Carl had worked with my dad forever, both on the farm and at the factory. I remember when I first found out he wasn't part of our family, it was a shock; all those years I had just assumed he was related to us.

My dad said, "Doug, go get us some of your mother's tea. Bring the whole jug out here." I imagined myself in an apron as one of the men teased me. "Yeah, Dougie, be a good girl and go get us something to drink." My dad ignored it, as he smoothed a section of concrete so expertly that it looked like murky glass. I returned lugging the iced tea with a stack of plastic cups under my arm. I passed around the cups and my dad poured each man a portion of the cold tea. I ran back to the house and brought out the sugar. Some men spooned in the glittery stuff as others simply gulped down the tea, sweat and tea staining dark spots on their shirts. I drank a hearty gulp as well, the taste bitter without the sugar I normally used and would've added had I not been in the men's presence. Jerry, a guy who scared me with his crazy eyes and comments about women's private parts, pulled a bottle from his hip pocket and started to pour a good stiff swig into his tea. He was six-foot-two and missing a few front teeth due to a couple of accidents at the factory. His forearms sported a jungle of tattoos. When he came to our house, he covered the tattoo on his right bicep of a curvaceous nude woman with a thick thatch of pubic hair, her face sad, her carmine lips parted as if to confess an unbearable truth. I'd seen her once and she was beautiful. It was the other ones that scared me, the skeleton on a black motorcycle going down in flames, or the letters on his knuckles that spelled out hate and love in faltering black ink.

My father had scolded Jerry in the past for his language, and now he gave him a tight-lipped glare. I caught the look and knew it was intended to keep me from seeing a man drinking during the day. On a few occasions, I'd seen my dad sip a beer or even have a mixed drink, but for the most part, he kept his family shielded from the sight of men drinking.

Jerry quickly tucked the nearly empty bottle back into his frayed jeans pocket and, attempting a diversion, raised his cup to toast, his wooly, matted-down underarm hair in full view. "Here's to Doug playing for IU!" I was self-conscious and acted as if I were still drinking my iced tea, faking swallows, keeping the glass to my lips. The basketball court was perfect, and I was eager to play on it, but more than anything, I was thrilled to have done a secret deed with my father.

In the distance, across from where the court was being built, was an old shed. At dawn, with the horizon golden above the barns, we'd snuck from the house to the shed—just me and my dad, our secret—and dug out an old metal box with chain and padlock. We slipped items into the box that we thought no one would miss and that represented 1981: a dollar bill, a picture of our family, a week-old copy of the *Wabash Plain-Dealer*, a cassette tape with a recording of an IU vs. Purdue game on it, a disposable razor, three nickels, and an empty pop bottle. We shrouded the items in plastic and locked the box. The smell of my father, two parts Old Spice and one part coffee, lingered in the shed as he turned to me and offered his hand. We shook hands and grinned at one another, conspirators in preserving our little, simple lives. Together we dug a hole in the sand and wedged the time capsule snugly into place. It wouldn't be long before the men would arrive. My dad and I stood on the freshly packed sand and looked at one another. He put his forefinger to his lips and said, "Shhhh. It's our secret."

. . .

Once the concrete was completely smooth, Jerry took me by the arm and led me to the edge of the wet court. "Ladies and gentlemen!" he announced, squeezing my mushy bicep as he said *ladies*. "We are gathered here today to honor one of b-ball's favorite sons. A shooter of shooters! The dribbler of all dribblers! Doug . . . 'the Hook' . . . Crandell!" The men clapped as Jerry hissed like an entire crowd and made a high-pitched whistle with just his thumb and forefinger.

Jerry continued to clutch my arm as he lowered me to a kneeling position. He took my hands, told me to splay them, and then gently pressed them into the cool, grainy cement. He yanked me up while the other men clapped again. "Sign it," he said, handing me a stick. I drew my initials near my right thumb. I was embarrassed; my handprints looked like those of a child's in a painting done in daycare.

Jerry puffed a cigarette and winked in my father's direction, an act I assumed was meant to say, "Don't worry, Dan, the boy will get bigger." I felt awkward after the clapping and started toward my dad. I tripped over dirt clods and broken rebar. When I was next to him, I wanted to hug him, or be hugged. Instead, we stood together and stared at the gray slab of cement, our secrets buried below.

OUR SACRIFICIAL CALVES

The Celotex factory was just about the only place to work in Lagro, employing roughly one hundred men and women from the surrounding little towns of Wabash County. It had been in operation for nearly seventy-five years when I went to work there, producing insulation board, ceiling tiles, and rock wool that was sent by train to factories around the country to manufacture all kinds of tile products. The production floor was about the size of a football field, with the remainder of the plant made up of two large warehouses and the wool mill, connected to the break and bathroom areas by a series of forklift alleys.

During my first week on the job, while peeing at a stall in the foul and dilapidated locker room, Jerry, the tattooed man who'd helped smooth my basketball court, said, "Your old man really helped me out Monday." He wasn't following the unspoken rule of staring straight ahead while pissing; in fact, he was leaning over the partition between us, trying to cop a peek, his bushy mustache gyrating side to side. "Damn, little man, that rod hasn't grown a bit." He shivered and zipped up, chuckling. I couldn't help but look down. "Relax," he said, "I'm just fucking with you." Jerry sucked in a gasp of breath and coughed as if barking. "Yep, ol' Dan saved me again. Got a mother hangover, and he took my shift." He went to the mirror and combed his thick hair with a yellow Goody comb, watching me in the mirror as he primped. "I sure wish I knew what that old boy takes to keep pulling so many. You look a little logy too, better get some caffeine pills before you doze off and get made into a ceiling tile." I almost laughed out loud at Jerry's comment; the notion that my father "used" anything except strong black Folgers seemed as ridiculous as Jerry ever being described as couth or polite. I turned to tell him just that, but he was gone.

I was scheduled to pull my first sixteen-hour shift that night. I hadn't seen my dad for any real length of time for several days; he had seniority and agreed to all the overtime he could get. My shift started at 4:00 P.M. and would end at 8:00 A.M. the next day. I was scheduled to work in the wool mill, where I would operate a simple baling machine that packed together fifteen-hundred-pound bales of rock wool to be sent to other factories. It was a tedious job that required the operator to sit and watch until it was time to flip a switch and drop a rubber block to separate one bale from another. The process took place in ten-minute intervals, the perfect amount of time to allow sleepiness to creep in and overtake the operator. If it happened, legend had it, that you did fall asleep on the job, the bale would become gigantic, a Moby, they called it. Rumor was a college kid fell asleep at the helm in the 1970s and produced a bale so large it took three forklifts to get it off the scales. But while the men joked about past Mobys, it was really no laughing matter. A bale that large meant more work for everyone. It had to be banded together by hand—a difficult task requiring several men—only to be hauled back to the rear of the baler to be broken up and fed through again.

The fear of a whale bale kept me on edge. I drank cup after cup of coffee and never sat down. Except for a furnace operator feeding the fire of slag behind me in the roaring cupolas, the only other workers were on the opposite side of the factory. The baler operator could work all night without talking to anyone. Every half hour or so a forklift driver came to haul the bales of rock wool off the line and into the backs of semis, but he was too busy to stop and chat.

That morning, after I clocked out, I drove home in the boxy 1979 Chevy Malibu my dad had bought to get back and forth to work. It had nearly bald tires, no air conditioning, and the front end was smashed in as if it had been hit head-on. It was the only vehicle my parents had. My first sixteen-hour shift had left me exhausted but wired, worn out but energized by caffeine, fueled by the way the morning looked after a long night's work—all pink and orange, the sun glistening through the trees. The curves on the back road were nearly overtaken by soaring, tawny ragweed growing in the ditches; the cornfields lined the ribbon of pavement in dark green. I steered the car through the many turns leading to the backside of the city of Wabash, where I'd drive a few blocks into town to the house my parents rented for $400 a month. It was a steel house built in the late 1970s. Made up of metal panels rather than wood or brick, it enclosed its inhabitants in a hot, constantly vibrating echo chamber.

The humid air blowing through the open car window held the scent of warming tar laced with silage vapors escaping from the many silos I passed. They stood like sentries on decrepit farms snuggled back away from the road, crannied into massive oak orchards, and surrounded by rusting, brown implements left where they'd died. My eyelids dipped. Twice my chin fell to my chest and then bounced up again as I tried to keep from dozing off. I gunned the motor, anxious to get home and act indifferent about my first long night when my dad asked how it went. My head dropped again when suddenly a blur of hurtling black flashed before the hood of the car. I slammed my boot hard onto the brake pedal as a thunderous impact threw my head back, caused the car to groan under the strain. My neck snapped forward as the car came to a halt.

Outside, it was quiet except for the slight buzzing of yellow jackets teetering on the tops of ditch mallow. I looked out and saw blood specks on the glass, a larger spot down near the pug-nose of the car. I realized I had a death grip on the steering wheel, my knuckles flour white, fingers bright pink everywhere else. I let loose of the wheel and opened the door, which made a metallic wrenching sound as I crawled out. I looked up and down the road and saw nothing, only the shimmer of heat rising from the pavement, creating a wavy mirage in the distance.

I walked to the wheel-well and braced myself, took a deep breath, and swung around the nose of the car. On the pavement, bleeding from its nostrils, lay a small steer, no more than a month old, maybe 100 pounds. I squatted down and rubbed its soft ears. Mercifully he was in no pain because the impact had killed the animal instantly, but that didn't keep me from feeling sick and awful.

I went to the back of the car and was about to open the trunk when I spotted a man walking calmly across the pasture. He waved unemotionally at me as his thin figure came closer and closer. I thought he'd be yelling by now, irate that I'd hit his livestock, but as he motioned toward a section of the barbed wire that separated us, pointing out a large hank of black hair, he said, "He was a jumper. Couldn't keep him in nowhere. Wasn't your fault. If you'll help me bury him we'll call it even." The old man stretched the fence to make an opening to crawl through himself. He had gentle blue eyes and a sad but pleasant expression on his tanned face.

Together we carried the poor little steer to the fence. The man said, "I'll get over on the other side and we'll slide him under the bottom." I pushed while he lifted and scooted his dead calf under the fence. His house was in the distance, about one hundred yards back in a nook of poplar trees and surrounded by soybean fields.

"You stay with him," the old man said, "and I'll go get a couple shovels." His concern for the calf and his calm manner soothed me. I watched as he made his way across the short grass toward the house and barns. Black cattle dotted the fence line further away, and several of them bawled at the sight of their owner, telling him they'd like some grain. I couldn't look down at the calf; a bee sting of hurt settled in my throat.

The old man came back with a shovel and a gunnysack. I was so tired I thought I could climb into the shallow grave with the baby calf and sleep forever, but there was something so familiar about my feelings. It was a story my father had told me about cattle.

. . .

In the fall of 1965, three years before I was born, Dan and Doris Crandell were not yet thirty. They lived with their three children, Derrick, Darren, and Dina, on a cash-rented farm called the Duffy Place. The couple had not yet managed to grab the slithering tail of their dream of farm ownership, but they were feeling hopeful. They had moved from Terre Haute to Greencastle and then to Northern Indiana with my dad's parents in tow at each relocation. My dad had convinced his father that buying twenty-five Angus steers would make them a profit if they fed them on the Duffy pastures. They argued over it several times, but my father had tallied up the amount that could be made by selling the steers and explained how that number would figure into the mathematics of a down payment on a farm. Finally, my grandfather agreed to help finance the steers.

My parents sat planning at the kitchen table. It was getting late, past midnight, so they decided to turn in, happy that the numbers showed that, with beef prices the highest in five years, they were ahead of schedule on getting their down payment saved.

Shortly after 3:00 A.M., my mother heard the phone ringing. Assuming it was just a fluke, she didn't get up to answer it. My father has always slept deeply and kept right on snoring. My mother tried to get back to sleep and drifted in and out of a dream before she woke again with a start, a pounding on the front door like a sledgehammer, she recalls.

"I went to the front door in my housecoat. There was a Wabash County sheriff and the Urbana town marshall. I couldn't believe what they were telling me. I thought I was dreaming. They said our steers had gotten out on the railroad tracks, and some were dead. I went and shook Dan awake and he went with the police."

My dad rode in the backseat of the cruiser to the covered tracks over the Wabash River. About fifteen of the black steers had gotten free of the fenced-in pasture and wandered on to the tracks over the river. When the locomotive sped toward the tunnel, there was no place for the cattle to go, and it was too late when the conductor used the horn to spook them back in the other direction. The train cut the cattle to pieces. There were legs and heads and hide on the tracks, pieces floating in the river. It was dark, so the sheriff gave my dad a flashlight to look for himself. It was raining, but even with all the water he could make out the blood in pools on the banks and in the river.

My father explained to the authorities what he thought had happened. He and his dad had been in constant debate with the railroad company to keep up their side of the fence that stretched over the flat space between the butte of the river and the pasture of the Duffy Place. They'd called the company and had been told it would be fixed time and time again. My grandfather had patched it the best he could, stringing extra barbed wire and weaving the holes with thick limbs. He even tied pie pans to the weak spots to scare off the curious steers. But it had not worked, and now, with the river swimming with cattle remains, my father saw his dreams sinking in the dark river as well. It was a long night for him. Before the sun came up and the fertilizer company dredged the river for the remains of his poor cattle, he rode back to the farm in the sheriff's car and stopped at my grandparents' house across the pasture. Knocking on the door at dawn, he felt terrible. He'd convinced his dad to move up north and had hounded him about the cattle purchase. Together they'd taken a loan out from the credit union to buy those steers, and now most of them were dead.

It would take over two years before the railroad company would pay out about half of what the cattle were worth. My grandfather wrote a letter to the editor of *Prairie Farmer* magazine asking for assistance in putting pressure on the railroad to pay up. It was considered weak for a farmer to ask for help, and when my dad recalls the death of his cattle on the railroad tracks, he's bothered most by having put his father in that position.

By midafternoon, the mess had been cleaned up and a truck had hauled off the steer parts to be ground up and used for fertilizer on some other farmer's fields. My father got a check for ninety dollars and drove his truck back home to the farm. He walked across the pasture to my grandparents' house. My grandfather had not said much when my father had told him about the cattle, but there was tension. My father knocked on the door for the second time since dawn. His mother answered and told him his father was down in the lower shed, working on a corn planter. My dad walked slowly down the hill to the shed, the fertilizer check in his hand. He found my skinny grandfather crawled up under the metal gears of the planter. My dad said, "I got it taken care of out there. Here's the check from the stink wagon." He placed the check under a toolbox. My grandfather said, "That's bad money. I don't want it." The check blew out from underneath the toolbox. My dad says they never cashed it, that it blew around the barn lot for a day or so. He'd see it stuck against a fence post or pinned under a clump of shit, and then it eventually vanished. My father, full of guilt and defeat, and badgered by his mother, began to do what he'd always felt he'd have to, look for a job off the farm. When his last two children were born in 1968 and 1969, he applied for a warehouse job at the Celotex factory. The prospect of living the life he'd dreamed of was slipping away. Now, he'd be bossed around, made to follow someone else's will, take orders.

.   .   .

We don't get desperate over one event, or even two or three; it's the continual pounding of our dreams that pushes us over the edge. As I helped the old farmer rake dirt over the calf's grave, I knew what I would do after I left him. I'd drive the car to the drug store and buy some NoDoz, and never tell a word of what had happened to my father.

4

INITIATION ON THE LINE

Days passed as my father and I shared silent car rides to and from work. I would spot him from time to time around the factory. Our overtime shifts, the ones that I now worked regularly, would overlap at midnight or 4:00 A.M. I'd watch him from afar as he emptied a monstrous Dumpster with just the tip of his forklift, shaking it wildly from his seat behind the wheel by rapidly tapping the controls, the thing dangling ten, fifteen feet in the air, dust and rock wool debris always blowing away from him, a calculation on his part. He was so good at his job, so strong; I still envied how easily he embodied manhood.

Since the incident with the calf, I'd taken to using caffeine pills regularly. I'd crush them up and dissolve the powder in a can of pop or a cup of coffee. I learned how many pills would keep my mind alert yet not make me jittery, a tough balance to strike when the double shifts would come as a surprise. Someone would call in sick or not show up for some reason, and I'd find myself starting the second eight hours without much notice.

One night I was asked to stay over in a job called board-feeder. Essentially, the job required the worker to use a device called a "dog" to retrieve the freshly baked and stacked sheets of long ceiling tile. From there the tiles were fed into a planer that started the squares down the fab line to be cut, beveled, and painted, heading for the packing department. The dog proved to be a cumbersome piece of machinery to master. It had a "tail," a metal handle that was used to guide it, but the controls worked in an opposite manner from how a car steers, causing newbies to really embarrass themselves while learning to operate it.

The board-feeder was responsible for keeping a steady supply of tile fed into the planer; in between, he sat on a stool for ten minutes, waiting before going after more. On a clipboard he recorded the lot number where the boards came from and the precise time they were fed into the planer. Before I started, Patsy, a man who rarely spoke but would imitate various dog barks on command, handed me his pencil. For some reason, several other men gathered around to watch me receive it. By now I was aware of some of the induction rites and rituals of factory life, and I should've known something was up. But I was wired on caffeine and preoccupied trying to figure out a way to crush up more NoDoz without anyone seeing me.

For several days the factory was full of rumors about a mysterious phenomenon. Men on the line were gossiping about *something* that was damaging whole boxes of packaged ceiling tile. A guy who'd had a nervous breakdown, nicknamed Money, told another man on the line, "I think it's a bloodthirsty ghost ripping those cartons up." He looked around as if he was afraid of being heard. "Just wait, they'll get us all before it's up."

For most of the shift, I sat idly on the stool, waiting for the next load of tiles to be fed into the line. In between, I retrieved skids with the dog. On one occasion, I tipped a whole skid over, busting up the raw boards that had just been pulled from the ovens. Their value was about two thousand dollars retail, and I thought I'd be fired. The caffeine pills had given me the jitters, but even without them I'm sure I would have tipped the skid over. I sucked at driving the dog, and it was a nightmare to stumble upon the thing somewhere in the factory.

At break Patsy, the other "dog" in the house, was commanded to perform. "Beagle!" his friend yelled, and Patsy wailed like a homesick pup weaned from its mother. I drank another pop and looked at the time clock; it was just after 4:00 A.M., and I felt I could make it through until dawn. I stood and stretched, the smell of cigarettes in the break room making my nose ache, the smoke hanging in the room like dense fog. The fifteen-minute breaks, hammered out in the contract, were only a tease. My back was knotted from sitting on the stool, and my right hand boasted a puffy sachet of blister; it covered my palm and was tinged with pink around the edges. I sat back down on the bench and waited for the break to end. Patsy was now into his schnauzer imitation, having received a standing ovation for his poodle and mutt. Patsy always wore the same pair of tight pants to work. They clung below his drooping gut, exposing a generous expanse of white ass crack. When he barked, howled, yapped, and growled, the pants would shimmy down a little, giving the unfortunate soul behind him an even clearer view of his pale cleft. But Patsy was far from shy about revealing himself, and if you paid attention you'd see him actually tugging covertly on the pants, trying to give his audience a treat. Patsy had also made the decision to forgo having a hernia operation, opting instead to use the bulge in his pants as a way to entice the ladies. Under the tight material, it looked as though a small throw pillow had been thrust down his trousers.

Since Patsy didn't speak anything but dog, one of his biggest fans, Larry, a guy with a pompadour that stood like a wave on his forehead, said, "Hey Patsy, little Crandell here still got your pencil?" Patsy barked and looked at me with his sad basset hound eyes.

I pulled the pencil from behind my ear and showed it to them. Patsy crooned a mixture of his helpful shepherd and playful wolf, meant to convey his pleasure at seeing his special pencil. Larry hee-hawed so hard his pompadour nearly came unglued. Patsy pretended to lick his paws and wag his tail. Some men in the factory avoided Patsy altogether, irritated by his decades-long role of the family pet, while others seemed unable to get enough. My dad was in the first category, but didn't come right out and say it.

The last four hours of the shift dragged on as if the hands on the large wall clock were stuck in place. Every once in a while I'd catch a glimpse of some of the men working the line, chuckling, then looking away quickly when I caught their gaze. I just assumed they were still getting a kick out of my ineptness at operating the dog and dumping over perfectly good product.

I was coming down off the NoDoz and felt it. It was a real quandary; if I took some more, I'd have difficulty sleeping, but if I didn't, I feared I'd hit another animal or person on the drive home, or shame my father by not being able to cut the work. So, right around 6:00 A.M. I popped three tablets while retrieving a skid in a remote section of the factory. I knew it meant no sleep, but I had two hours to go and wanted to make certain I could work the sixteen and then some.

When the bell finally rang, ten minutes before eight, I was relieved not to have screwed up any more skids. Sitting on the stool all night absentmindedly fiddling with the clipboard and pencil was brutal. I disliked the job and hoped I could find a way not to have to pull overtime on it again.

In the bathroom I cleaned up, washing my face and dusting off my clothes. I looked in the mirror as Jerry hobbled in, already pulling his penis from his fly before even getting near the stall. He acted as if he didn't see me and made a loud and expressive sigh of relief as he whizzed out what sounded like gallons, and then let out several painful-sounding farts.

"You look a little wired, Dougie," he said, an accusatory tone mixed with a hint of camaraderie in his voice. I didn't speak. He came over to the sink, a wild look of anger and hope in his eyes. His tattoo of the naked lady, the one I'd found so pretty as an adolescent, now seemed vulgar; it appeared to pulse on his skin, the ink fading into his pores as if she was leaving him, drilling her apparition nearer his bone, trying to hide from her dangerous owner.

Jerry scrubbed his face until it was glowing red, and I should've left, but something in me sensed a purpose. Jerry had always intrigued me, even if I saw him as too raw, too willing to say things others only thought. I never knew what he was going to do next.

He toweled off as we made small talk, and then without introduction he said, "Here, don't tell your old man," as he slipped me a trio of expertly rolled joints and left the bathroom, the strong smell of his urine still floating in the air.

In the break room we all waited in line, listening to the subtle ticks that meant we were closer to going home. Patsy scratched at the back door and whined. Larry, with his high wedge of coal locks, jumped at the chance to let in the factory pet. Men in line began to laugh harder and harder, even the ones that normally hated to see Patsy trotting along. They eyed me and laughed even harder, the same way they'd done during the whole shift.

Two minutes before clock-out time Larry led his pooch right up to me and said, "Patsy needs to put his pencil back from where it came." With that Patsy got down on all fours, his butt crack exposed as I handed the pencil from behind my ear to Larry, who quickly, with just the slightest of pauses for dramatic effect, placed it into the dog's greasy ass cheeks. The men roared. With the whole shift replaying in my head, I recalled how I'd fiddled with the pencil, carried it behind my ear, held it, and, God forbid, chewed on it. The laughter drowned out the time clock buzzing, and the few men who had no interest in the rite of passage began to file out. Jerry lumbered past me and stopped momentarily before shoving his time card into the slot. "Be glad you got three amigos to help you see the humor in that," he said, referring to the joints he'd given me. Patsy was still on all fours, sniffing the floor and milking the crowd for the very last drops of laughter, Larry using a pretend leash to keep him from running off. In less than an hour, I'd smoke one of the joints and sleep soundly for the first time in days, the burnt marjoram smell like a soothing tea, allowing me to feel hungry and calm. I'd worked at the factory for just under a month, and already I found the long hours to be a demonic force, making you do things you'd never dreamt of. The double shifts left you without a center, day and night bleeding together. Living with my parents again seemed like defeat. Work was all there was, and its time was always near, never really over, continuously beginning.

WE'RE GOING LOONEY TUNES

My mother had been a handful for my father ever since her emergency surgery when I was seven years old. When the doctor told her she'd had a hysterectomy, she didn't know what the word meant. So he said simply, "You're done having children." For months afterward she was sullen and acted strangely. She did not receive any postoperative care, and the doctor never considered hormone replacement therapy. My mother began talking in the third person seemingly from out of nowhere; but it was clear she was using it as a coping strategy, a way to distance herself from what was happening around her. In short, she was telling stories, where her involvement was narrated through the safety of "she" and "her" rather than the terrifying "I."

She would take on projects way too large to complete, like painting walls with intricate details (without approval from the landlord) in one of the many rental houses we occupied, or plowing up the entire backyard to plant a new type of russet potato. My dad did what he could to help her, but she preferred to sew and craft rather than do just about anything else, losing herself in projects for days, even weeks. She hopped from one food service job to another, and at each stop she found ways to incorporate her crafting skills, such as making life-sized renditions of popular promotional characters: Smurfs, Raggedy Ann and Andy, Cabbage Patch Kids, and the occasional George Washington or Abraham Lincoln if the sale on cheddar melts happened to fall on President's Day.

In the metal house, she asked if I'd model Sylvester the Cat for her. "Honey, I can't tell if your mother's got his tail centered. Will you put it on so she can see?" I looked up from a bowl of Cheerios, my head light and fuzzy, a woozy mixture of the weed and caffeine. "Please," she insisted, a weak smile on her face, rubber thimbles capping most of her fingers. I stood up and took the black felt suit from her hands. It looked as though it had been deflated, a human-sized cat with no musculoskeletal system to fill it out. I agreed. What can I say, I've never been able to tell the woman no, even if that meant my own humiliation. She'd sewn clothes for me when I was a kid. Once, she made me a pair of pajamas that had pink lace around the neck. I wore them. Another time she made a pair of polyester pants for me that could only be described as girls' hip-huggers. I was ten, and I wore them too.

My father was in the bedroom snoring, amplified by the metal construction of the rented house. I'd swear at times the whole buzzing structure was about to come tumbling down. In the bathroom I pulled on the Sylvester suit. It was a nearly perfect rendition except that Doris was right, the tail was off-center, nearly on my hip, actually. The head covering was outstanding; it came with fish-line whiskers, a set of finely crafted ears, and a chin strap that held it all in place. The doors in the house were also made of steel, and they recessed into the metal walls. I slid the door open and stepped out wearing the Looney Tunes garb. My father, awake now and needing to pee, nearly ran into me. His little hairy friend was not sitting on top of his head, and the skin there shone soft and vulnerable, like a baby's.

He rubbed his eyes and looked me up and down. For a second, I thought he might just punch me right in the face, but he only grunted and stepped around me. When he slid the bathroom door shut behind me, it sounded like a cage door closing.

I walked to the tiny kitchen, where my mother was fixing coffee. She counted out loud the number of scoops she spooned into the filter basket. She heard my furry feet brushing against the Berber carpet and turned to survey me. She said, "That tail shouldn't be that far over," as if commenting on some heretofore unknown fact. She scooted toward me and took hold of the tail, tugged on it to try and put the thing in the right place. It didn't work. She tugged harder and ripped the tail clean off Sylvester's ass. "Oh, no," she said, "your mother's ripped it off."

"Really?" I said. She stood before me holding the tail, a look of dismay on her face, as she held it just below her nose, the white stuffing poking out the end, as if she were about to sniff it. "Give me that," I said, smiling at her. She looked tired and jittery, worried.

I went to the pantry and stripped off the Sylvester outfit, pulling on my jeans and work boots. My mother called into me, "Your mother made Porky the Pig, Bugs Bunny, and Tweety Bird too. It's for a promotion at Arby's. Some of my teenagers are going to wear them to help sell those new glasses with all the cartoon characters on them." I could only imagine how some poor kids from Wabash must be feeling, knowing they'd have to clock in that day and have my mother, their manager, suit them up in the god-awful outfits and prance them out to the curb to wave people into the store.

At the table I sat down to drink some coffee. My father had stayed in the bathroom for almost an hour, showering, shaving, and gluing down his toupee. When he finally came out, he smelled of hot water, bar soap, and Stetson cologne. The three of us sat at the table sipping coffee. In less than two hours my dad and I would have to be back at the factory for at least twelve hours, possibly sixteen. It was quiet, save for the clicking sounds of the coffeemaker behind us. Outside, the sun beat down, burning up my mother's geraniums. She'd given up on trying to keep them alive, opting instead to pick the dandelions sprouting in the lion-colored lawn. By bunches she'd bring them in, clutching them to her chest as she filled a Folgers can with water.

Sitting in silence at the table, I watched my mother staring at my dad, a look of weariness in her eyes. It appeared as though she was about to say something to him when the phone rang. My dad stood up, knocking the spoon from his saucer, and went to answer it. My mother's eyes filled with tears, expecting, I thought, for it to be another of his secretive phone calls. I acted as though some creamer needed mixing inside my cup. When my dad returned to the table he was visibly rattled, lips clamped tightly shut, his brow furrowed.

"That was the union rep." My dad swallowed hard, and said, "Carl accidentally ran over one of the twins last night with the mower. She's dead." My mother openly sobbed, burying her face in her hands. It was as if she caught herself feeling relief then utter remorse, her emotions in a tight brawl. She quickly stood and began ridding the table of our unfinished coffees. The twins had wanted to be near their dad as they always did, and had begged Carl to let them ride on the tractor with him. With his perfect ten-year-old girls on either side of him, their little legs dangling off the wheel wells, Carl cut first one swath, then another, as the Bush Hog reduced the tall brush to tiny chips. At the end of the field, the tractor bumped over a deep furrow and the whole assembly bounced back and forth. One of the twins lost her grip and slipped, fell off the tractor and under the mower. It would have been impossible to avoid running over her.

My father looked as if the air had been let out of him. My mother clinked dishes against one another, the hot water in the sink running rapidly as she scrapped at saucers that didn't need it, and let out tiny sobs like she was dying.

I hoped my dad might find a way to talk out what he was feeling, but instead, he stood and walked to the door to pick up his keys and wallet on a stand. "Some of us are going over there now," he said loudly enough for my mother to hear in the kitchen. I stood to go along, but my dad stopped me. "You've gotta fill in at the factory. I told them you'd be right over. Someone's gonna pick you up." With that he left the house. I stood there feeling queasy, anger riding up too. From the kitchen my mother sniffled, "Thank you, baby, for trying on the cat. Pray for Carl's family. Your mother's going to right now." When I left the house, she was out back, picking dandelions that had already gone to seed.

. . .

Word spread about Carl's horrible accident. The factory mourned. I learned that these men, who could say some of the crudest things, were also capable of intense empathy. They'd walked picket lines together, fought together to get an extra dime of medical coverage, and attended one another's weddings and burials. The same man who had over the years developed hard feelings toward another man, because of a job bid loss or a shift preferential, could come to his aid, help feed his family.

I clocked in and quickly went to the bathroom to swallow several caffeine pills. I was due at my station in ten minutes. As I left the stall to wash up at the sink, a man nicknamed MF, short for "motherfucker," came into the bathroom, his clothes riddled with rock wool, so much so that he appeared to have been tarred and feathered. His real name was Henry, and like many of the men working at Celotex, he'd done time in prison. The factory, like a high school, had its cliques: ex-cons, Vietnam vets, born-agains, farmers, and younger men they called lifers—guys that started out working for college money then ended up staying on, trapped. Celotex was one of the few places in town that paid decent wages and offered some security. Being called a lifer was a put-down, something that implied you'd fucked up and passed on an education. I was terrified of the term.

Henry said, as he tried in vain to rid his coveralls of the rock wool, "They moved you, son." Tiny clumps of the wool swarmed around him as he swatted and pawed at his clothes, running his fingers through his fluffy hair to keep the fine filaments from nestling into his scalp and forming a painful version of dandruff.

"You're gonna be over in the wool plant with me. I'm going on sixteen too." He hadn't improved the condition of his clothes much, even with all the effort, and he left the bathroom with a toothless smile, his coveralls still peppered with wool. I was glad not to have to be on the other side of the factory, the part that fabricated the boards, where the evil "dog" resided and where the other dog, Patsy, would be whimpering to indicate sorrow. The wool mill is where I preferred to work in solitude, with only a few men like MF around, good-hearted drunks and past offenders, men whose crusty exterior disguised what truly lay underneath.

At the baler I swept up and then called the foreman on the other side of the plant to let him know the conveyor was full of bales. Soon I heard a forklift barreling in my direction. It was my dad. We saw little of each other at the factory. I'd hoped working near him would offer us a chance to bond, become buddies, but the hope had turned to something else—a kind of dread.

He zipped past me at the baler and never looked my way. At the end of the conveyor he expertly plucked the huge bales with the shiny forks as if they were as light as the hazy air. I erected my posture and continued to sweep up, feigning indifference. Every few minutes he'd fly back into the mill with speed and precision, taking three bales at a time. It was widely known that he was a master at filling the train cars. My dad loved being around the trains. I suspect it had something do to with their destinies, that they were going places while he had to stay put. When we were little, and he'd only been working at the factory a few years, he would bring home items that had fallen off the train. Once, he toted home a huge cardboard box full of Goody barrettes. Inside there was every size and shape of hair doodads. My little sister clipped a whole mess of them into my cropped bangs and along the crown of my head. I loved it but knew it was wrong for a boy to wear them. At dinnertime, when our mother called us, my sister and I made sure to take them all out, but we missed one: a bright pink barrette held my hair off my right ear. When I realized it later at the table I ripped the thing out so fast it took hair with it.

My dad appeared from around the back of the baler, his cheeks slightly red, a pair of worn leather gloves tight on his fists, his shirtsleeves rolled up like a Depression-era boxer's.

He walked with a Styrofoam cup to the giant Igloo cooler and filled the cup with yellow Gatorade. The union contract stipulated plenty of water and Gatorade when the temperature in the factory rose above 100 degrees, which it did almost every day during the Indiana summer. He sucked down a cup and filled it again. He wiped his mouth like John Wayne and tossed the cup into the dustbin. I felt as yellow as the Gatorade, cowardly, unable to connect with him.

He had to yell to be heard over the cupolas. "I'm here for sixteen too. Load out. Buzz me on the phone when the conveyor is full and I'll take care of it." I nodded my head. He turned to go and I had to almost scream myself. "How's Carl?" My dad swung around, angry. He took me by the arm and ushered me to a quieter spot near some lockers. "Goddamn it," he said, fire in his voice, "be fucking careful over here. That piece-of-shit baler locks up, don't you get up there like Henry does and try and unjam it. Call the goddamn foreman. It's his job. Don't you do it!" He let loose of the tight grip on my arm, my body slumping away, my face red from being berated. I turned my back on him and began sweeping. I heard his forklift roar to life and he sped away, only to return in a couple minutes.

He pulled up alongside of the baler and shut off the engine, yelled, "Son, you need any money for lunch?" I shook my head no, and for a moment I thought I could see him about to break—a slight quiver in his chin, perhaps some glassy eyes. He paused, looking as though he were trying to find some of the precious words he kept so much to himself. I looked away to give him a chance, but it wasn't going to happen. His best friend was going through hell, and it was too much to believe my dad could find the words to explain it. No one could. Carl, the man I believed was an uncle, part of the family, would have to live the remainder of his life knowing he'd run over and chopped up his own baby. Those are the words my dad couldn't get to come out, so vulgar and true and altogether necessary.

The night wore on like a dull ache. Just off the docks, trains blasted by all night, horns roaring like tortured beasts. The rock wool kept coming to life, the machinery working with oiled exactitude, inch by inch pushing forth a new bale onto the scales for me to measure, weigh, record, then send down the conveyor. By midnight I could feel the weight of sleep. I'd pulled sixteens all month and hadn't slept well when I was supposed to, and now, as I watched the baler just starting on a new bale, I thought I'd simply close my eyes for a moment, rest my head on a sheath of insulation behind the rickety chair. There would be plenty of time before I'd need to band the bale, fifteen minutes, maybe more; besides, I was just resting my eyes anyway. . . .

. . .

When I got a really good look at the thing, after waking up and shoving my way past the other men, I had to admit it was something special. It was true, seeing it was like spotting a great white whale. The hump back, the grand girth, even the length lived up to its name: a Moby. Men brayed like jackasses as they slapped my back. Patsy had heard the news and ran over from the fab line to sniff it. Now, he lifted his leg, acted as if he were marking his territory. Men feeding the fiery cupolas edged forward from the red infernos behind them, inspecting my Moby with awe and pity. While the individual sheaths that made up the bale were tightly compacted, it was unbound, and to do anything with it, sell it or haul it away to be fed back into the baler, it would have to be banded. The orange flames melting the rocks one hundred feet away could not have been any hotter than my face. As the men dispersed, Henry and the other wool mill rats working high on the catwalks climbed down and came to my rescue. I was told to cut metal bands as long as the plant floor. "We're gonna have to double the sons-a-bitches," Henry said, a softness in his voice, trying to comfort me by not overreacting. I felt solid dread in my chest, and thought for certain that the foreman would find out. The men helping me take care of the enormous bale were thinking exactly what I was: my father would have to be the one to expertly maneuver my whale off the conveyor.

For over an hour we worked on the colossal production of my cat-nap, and by the time we were through the monster was contained. All that was left to do was get an accurate weight for the mythical record books. It weighed in at nearly 3,000 pounds, outdoing the last college kid's fuck-up by nearly a half-ton. I used an extra-large permanent marker to record the weight on the side of the bale as the other men went back to their own jobs. The fumes from the marker settled around my head. I'd just picked up the phone to dial my dad's extension when the line crackled and went silent. Over the loudspeaker the foreman cleared his throat. The fab line on the other side of the factory whined down, groaning into silence.

"If we could all please use the next couple of minutes of silence to pay respect to Carl Phelps and his family." With that the speakers went dead, and I hung my head, taking my cue from the men up in the catwalks. I craned my neck to look at them, and with the snowy puffs of rock wool swirling about their heads, I could've sworn they had sprouted wings, angelic in their towering roost, heads bent as they moved their lips.

When Carl would come to our farm to load livestock with my dad, they'd goose each other, but mostly it was my father doing the honors, tickled by how his short friend would blush, jump in the air, and yell, "Stop it, goddamn it!" Carl would be laughing so hard, and my dad too, and they'd feed off one another's laughter until they had stomachaches. Carl would come back to the factory, but I'd never see him smile again. Someone said, "He's dead behind his eyes. Nothing's there anymore." And it was true, Carl came to work, clocked in, and did his job, but his face was blank and pale. Even his body seemed to be on autopilot, performing tasks for a paycheck, but not really alive.

The period of silence was over and the hum of the fab line escalated, building energy, roaring back to life. The next step in the bereavement process of the union men was to gather cash from everyone for delivery to the family along with a gravesite wreath. At break that night a fat envelope was sealed and handed over to a steward. But now, as I was about to pick up the phone again, my dad flew up on his forklift. He shut the engine off and let the thing coast, stepping out of the seat as it rolled to a stop like a cowboy sliding easily from a trotting mare.

He approached me wearing a hesitant smile on his face, but it quickly faded, to show that he wasn't pleased with my birthing a whale, but also out of respect for his friend's loss. "Come on," he said, "I'll show you how to get this thing moved and fed back in before the foreman sees it." I felt relieved to have his help, but when I walked along with him I got a whiff of the sweet smell of alcohol that eased from his mouth. I couldn't help but notice how the steps we took were completely in sync.

PORTRAIT OF A BOY JOURNALING

Shortly after the factory men finished my basketball court, I was sent off to get a better jump shot. My father walked into the gymnasium at Lancer basketball camp in Winona Lake, Indiana, wearing his cuffed jeans and a blue chambray work shirt, the sleeves rolled up in perfect packets above his elbows, exposing his hairy arms and deep tan. I sat with other boys my age, twelve-year-olds with bad haircuts and little tribes of pimples invading their T-zones. From my seat I watched my father.

The last day of the camp was an exhibition in which we were to scrimmage and partake in all manner of contests: free throws, jump shots, defense, ball handling, and rebounding. Awards were to be handed out to the boys who performed these feats with the most precision. The night before, we'd been made to polish the maple bleachers, rubbing and shining the wood into a high-gloss sheen to hold the bottoms of our families when they came to watch us. I couldn't sleep that night, worrying that I wouldn't perform well and would disappoint my father. I'd practiced on the new court but couldn't use my left hand to dribble or shoot a layup.

My dad was a lefty and could shoot a hook shot that smacked the backboard with such force it sounded like thunder, then a slice of electric lightning as the ball swished through the net. He only had one pastime, other than reading the *Prairie Farmer*, and that was watching Indiana University, Notre Dame, and Purdue play college basketball, and he did it with zeal. We'd plan family nights around the televised games, popping corn and eating our dinners in front of the TV set. IU was his favorite, and together we hummed along with the fight song.

As I lay in my bunk bed the night before the exhibition, I fidgeted under the sheet and tossed and turned. Unable to sleep, I got up and went to the little desk, pulled the cracked shade down tight so I wouldn't wake my roommates. At orientation each boy had been given a notebook that contained diagrams of the campus, the camp rules, and line drawings of how to best block out under the bucket or how to flip one's wrist to ensure a full and snappy follow-through. In the back section of the notebook there was a weekly calendar with lines for making notes. I'd filled mine in daily despite the mocking of my teammates but had resisted the urge to fill in a section titled "The Future—What Are Your Goals?" But my sleeplessness had given me an excellent excuse to write in my notebook, and with a black Bic I began to answer each of the fifteen questions about what kinds of opportunities I thought lay before me. *Where do you see yourself in one year? Two? How about five? How does teamwork fit into your daily life? What makes a young man do the right thing?* I wrote and wrote in my slanted cursive writing, digging the tip of the pen deeply into the paper as I told my secret dreams to the notebook.

The camp director had a slim face and sunken eyes. His face wore the kind of worn-out look so many Midwestern fathers wear, an expression of desperate hope and whittled-down expectations. At the beginning of the camp he had discussed the contents of the note-book. I listened attentively as he went through each section and read it aloud. "This last section here," he said, as he thumbed through the pages at the end, "it's just there for notes. Don't worry about it, just make sure you know the rest." He had dismissed the section I found the most interesting, but I didn't want any of the other boys to know, so I had feigned disinterest. But at that dark little cubby under the lamp light, I let it all out. I wrote about things I'd never mentioned to anyone, how I didn't feel good about myself, how I couldn't imagine a time or place where I'd feel like a real man, and the trite thoughts I had about God.

It was well past 2:00 A.M. when I finished my journaling. My hand was cramped, and black ink was smeared from the tip of my pinky down along the edge of my palm. I closed my notebook gently and switched off the light. I remained seated at the desk and listened to the hum of the window fan. I can't recall how I got myself in bed that night, but in the morning, when our camp counselor thumped like a warden on the door, I sat up quickly and pulled the notebook out from beneath my pillow. For an instant, I thought of tossing it into the trash can or hiding it under the mattress, but instead I made sure to keep it in sight as I dressed for exhibition day, watching it carefully so that none of my roomies could try to snag it away.

As we filed into the gymnasium we turned in our notebooks to have the certificates in them stamped with a completion All-Star symbol. Once we stretched and warmed up, it was time to perform. My stomach hurt and I had gas, which seemed to slip out whenever I made a pass or took a shot.

I zigzagged down the court, dribbling poorly with my left hand, and was relieved to make it to the end without tripping over my own feet. My father sat on the bleachers with his legs spread, back erect. The camp director blew his whistle and gathered us together in the center of the court, where we divided into teams and started a fifteen-minute scrimmage. I missed a layup and threw the ball to a kid on the other team—right to him, directly into his hands. His shirt had confused me, and he scored easily as I chased after him in vain. If my father was disappointed he didn't show it, and before long the exhibition was over.

We were dismissed to go sit with our parents. The sharp chirps of our tennis shoes across the floor sounded like a multitude of alarms. The camp director rolled a podium with a microphone onto the shiny floor. His staff set up tables with trophies: 1st, 2nd, and 3rd place in each category. I could feel my cheeks redden as I plopped down next to my father. He smiled and quickly squeezed my bare knee, then retracted his hand as if I'd shocked him with static. My mother was all smiles and bragged on how my hair didn't mess up when I ran down the court. The lights in the gym dimmed, and a spotlight beamed down from above our heads and into the center of the court. The camp director tapped the microphone, and his seventeen-year-old son, who had the furriest thighs I'd ever seen, asked us to bow our heads. The kid spoke clearly and succinctly about the grace of God and the price of salvation and thanked the Lord for bringing all the families to the camp safely. I peeked over at my father, who sat stone-faced, looking out onto the floor as if watching a game. In unison the crowd chanted "Amen."

The camp director gave a brief introduction to the award categories. I knew I wasn't going to win anything, so I pretended to be preoccupied with my shoelaces as other boys left the bleachers to go retrieve their award. Near the end, all of us were called down to receive our participation ribbons, a gesture to keep the few of us who'd not landed a pretty trophy from feeling bad. One by one boys stepped forward and took the red ribbons with gold lettering already flaking off, and were given back our notebooks. But when it came my turn, I received only the ribbon. I climbed dutifully back into the stands to sing the national anthem, but I was crushed. What had happened to my journal? Had it been turned over to a highly trained psychologist for analysis? I just knew I'd be asked to stay afterward with my parents to discuss my troubled state of mind.

The music for the anthem started and my father put his strong hand over his heart and removed his cap. I'd never heard him sing before, and while his voice was deep and corded with cigarettes, I knew where I'd gotten my inability to carry a tune. He was so off that even he could hear it and began to sing lower, trailing off almost completely before it was over.

The camp director gave the signal to switch the lights back on, and the whole gymnasium flittered with fluorescence. I peered down onto the empty trophy tables and spotted my notebook. I wanted to run down and grab it and sprint out the gym doors into the country-side, away from my parents and the bigger boys with their hulking trophies.

The podium was about to be wheeled away when one of the college-aged staff took the camp director's arm and whispered into his ear, pointing at my notebook lying conspicuously on the bare table. My father had already stood up and had replaced his cap. The camp director walked slowly to the table and picked up the notebook, inspected it with disinterest. He wearily stepped back in front of the microphone. He coughed and flipped the switch back on.

"Excuse me folks," he said with edgy insistence. "We left some-thing out here." Silence. My dad sat back down while my mother pressed a Kleenex to her lips.

The camp director held the notebook in the air and declared unenthusiastically, "We give an award every year for the boy who best completes the section of his notebook in the back." He looked the notebook over before opening the cover and reading into the microphone, "Doug Crandell?" he asked, popping his head up. "You wanna come down here and get your trophy?" I heard the words but couldn't believe them. My mother squealed and clapped as I trod down the steps and onto the floor. The camp director handed me a wee little trophy the size of a teacup and flashed a gratuitous smile. I turned and tucked my notebook under my armpit and carried my trophy back up into the stands.

On the ride home, my mother asked me to read some of what I'd written, but I changed the subject to how the camp's food didn't taste nearly as good as hers. The tiny trophy sat against my pale thigh as my dad drove well over the speed limit back to Wabash. He was due at the factory at 4:00 P.M. My eyes lingered on his meaty hands wrapped around the pickup's steering wheel; they seemed to take up nearly all the space. I'd won something with my words, and he'd not said anything except, "That's good work." I'd sensed his confusion, his bafflement at the last-minute award. Sometimes I believed my father thought I talked too much, used too much of my time daydreaming. He was quiet, and even though I tried hard not to jabber on about something, I always failed.

At the driveway, my father shut the engine down, and the three of us sat in the truck. He looked at me and winked, unsure of what his role was in this situation. He said, grabbing my knee playfully, "You got ya' a trophy." He smiled and told my mother he'd just eat something out of the machines at the factory, as he fired the truck up again, a cue that we were to get out. I watched his truck disappear over a hill in the lane, the motor rapping, and the tiny trophy at my hip.

I've often wondered what went through his head that afternoon, driving from the farm to the factory, the notion that his son had won something for a commodity he conserved with the utmost frugality. I do recall what I was thinking. As I sat alone in my room, clutching my little trophy and rereading the sections I'd written, my mother downstairs cooking up a big supper, I felt, for the first time in my life, a calling, the sense that I'd been put together for some specific reason, some work that wouldn't involve just my weak body.

JAWS ON SPEED

It was as if my Moby never existed. The sighting was over, and the great beast had been fed back into the baler. My body was drained, and as I checked the baler, I sensed someone standing behind me. I wheeled around and was face-to-face with someone wearing the foam head of the shark from *Jaws*, clearly a reference to my whale hatching. From the corner of my eye I caught movement near a stack of skids, and snickering erupted into knee-slapping hee-haws, a whole group of men hiding, watching for my reaction. I reached to pull the costume head off, but whoever was wearing it slapped at my hand. I shot my hand up again, and this time the shark delivered a painful snag and twist of my wrist with combat precision. I knew then that it had to be Jerry. A tour in Vietnam had made him edgy and lightning-quick; besides, I could see the fading woman on his arm. He was easy to anger, especially with others watching. I decided to turn away, but he caught me by the nape of the neck and pushed me hard away from him, hurtling me headlong into the end of the baler scales, the steel corners sharp as any box knife. I hit my shin. Pain shot up my leg, and I could feel blood flowing.

The men hiding behind the skids took off in separate directions and Jerry stood motionless in his Jaws head, the cold black foam eyes locked on me as I pulled up my pant leg to take a look. He hadn't meant to hurt me, just humiliate me a bit in front of his audience. I hopped to the workstation and found some leftover McDonald's napkins and proceeded to pack them onto the cut. It was deep but wouldn't need stitches. Jerry took a step in my direction, but then thought twice. "Sorry," he said in a muffled voice, the fins on the costume head flapping. I shook my head yes, indicating I wasn't sore. He turned and began a quick walk then a jog as he headed to the other side of the plant. I knew he was scared I'd tell my dad.

I tied a piece of twine around the outside of my pant leg to hold the napkins on the cut and moved the first bale onto the scales. Once it was sent on its way I went to my lunch bag and pulled out a Coke and placed an envelope from Ball State University on the workstation table. I held the envelope up to the light to make sure I wouldn't tear the contents then gently peeled the end open and plucked the paper out. It said I'd been accepted for the last summer class I needed to finish my bachelor's degree in psychology. I hadn't a clue what I was going to do with the degree, but I would be the only person in my family to graduate from college, and the last class would be easy, even if I'd have to fit it around the long work hours.

I folded the envelope and tucked it into my back pocket. Another bale was inching forward when the phone rang. I heard Jerry's voice clearly: "Meet me out back by the railroad tracks after you get your next bale out. I got something for you." The phone went dead. I tried to convince myself I wouldn't be in any danger out in the dark with him, but still, I wondered if Jerry was going to punch me, drag me onto the tracks and tie me there for a train to come chugging by and make it look like some silly joke gone awry. But I knew he had more of what I needed, and I was willing to take the risk. I'd smoked the last two joints Jerry had given me, hiding behind the garage of the steel house, puffing as fast as I could, willing myself to eat and relax. I was hesitant at first, but the marijuana had temporarily fixed what was broken in me.

I sent the bale down the conveyor and looked around to make sure the coast was clear; it was insubordination to leave your post, even if your job was episodic. It was a rule loosely enforced, but I was temporary help and might be made an example of by the foreman. I walked quickly across the cement floor to a sliding door, rusty and crumbling, a line of sienna dust like an oblong anthill along the flimsy base. I jumped off the dock into a patch of tall fescue; it exploded with crickets, foolishly jumping into the spaces between the railroad ties. Something rustled in the ocher light blandly illuminating a hidden space to my right, a little cubbyhole where a deep shadow fell inward toward the building.

"Come here, Crandell," the voice said. I crept along, expecting at any minute to have to wrestle Jerry to the ground and bite his wrist. "Down here, man." I stumbled over one of the large stones that bordered each side of the tracks. I stopped briefly to look around; the sump pump kicked on in the lagoon and I could see car headlights steadily going in both directions on the highway across the field. The humid night air smelled of freshly mowed grass and the spoor of a hit skunk. A feral, half-grown kitten jumped from a ledge. I screamed. "Christ," I heard a voice say. "You gonna pee in your panties, Crandell?"

I was a step or two in front of the cubby entrance when Jerry slipped from the hole and stood before me in the dark, his silhouette laughable: a paunch at his belt and Popeye arms like swollen triangles sprouting from his upper body. His body had morphed into middle age, not at all like the man who'd worked on the basketball court. I hadn't noticed until now.

I smelled beer. In the dark, Jerry nonchalantly thrust a cold one into my unready hand and I dropped it. "You shithead," he said, "now it'll go everywhere." He stooped to pick it up from the ground and disappeared into the hole to exchange it.

"You think you can keep a hold of this one, Slippery Noodle?" He snorted a laugh as I took it and popped the tab.

He took big gulps from his sweaty can and I did the same. The cold beer flooded my throat and tasted excellent, bitter and icy. We finished them quickly and chugged two more each. My eyes watered and I interrupted the other noises—chirping crickets and mutant bullfrogs croaking on the banks of the polluted lagoon—with a deep, gravelly belch. Jerry did the same, blowing his exhale in my direction. "Can you smell my Wheaties from breakfast?"

"That's gross, Jerry," I said, sounding uptight.

"Aren't you gonna ask?" said Jerry, his voice low and conspiratorial.

Feeling the buzz, I said, "What? Are you gonna push me again, Jerry?" I said his name with a singsong lilt.

"Fuck you if you're gonna be that way," he said, real hurt in his voice.

"OK," I said, "seriously, what is it?" I didn't want to offend him, or risk missing out on more free weed.

Pouting, he shoved his hands into the filthy front pockets of his worn, paper-thin corduroys. How he wore the things in the dead heat of an Indiana summer was beyond me, but he liked them and had several pairs, all nearly in a state of disintegration.

"I was just joking. Sorry," I said. Jerry's mood changed entirely as he beamed a rotten smile.

"Come here," he whispered, and we ducked into the hiding place. Jerry fished into his shirt pocket, withdrew a silver lighter, flipped the lid open with a snap, and struck a flame. The orange flicker shone on his cupped palm. He had black grease on the tips of his fingers as if he'd been recently printed and booked for a crime. Jerry stooped and opened a cooler, pulled out a plastic baggie, and held it up for me to see.

"What do you think?"

"I don't know. What are they?"

"Speed. Clean and good. This stuff is much better than those caffeine pills you been taking." I didn't bother to ask him how he knew; Jerry had used so much in his life at the factory and at home that he could diagnose anyone. I made myself forget what he'd said about my dad, about him using something to pull so many sixteens.

"So?"

"So," said Jerry, unsure of why I was acting so stupid. "So, dumbass, you take these and you can work all night. No more of those Moby bales. But fuck, if you wanna keep fucking up, fine with me." He snapped the lighter shut and the space went dark.

"Wait," I said, "I didn't mean that." I couldn't see Jerry smile, but I knew he was; I could feel his energy change. I'd known Jerry for most of my life, and while he was sometimes cruel, I knew he really believed he was helping me. And after all it was my choice; I could've declined the offer.

"You sure they're safe?" I asked, taking a handful of pills from Jerry's wet hand and shoving them in my front pocket. Jerry popped us two more beers and looked at his Indiglo watch. "You got about five more minutes, Dougie." I took the can he offered and we gulped down rapid swigs. "Damn," he continued, "you gonna share those or not?" Together we popped a pill and drank the last of the beers. "This goddamn place is like that song 'Hotel California,'" said Jerry, waxing philosophical. I stopped and listened impatiently, scared I'd be found out if I didn't get back inside. He continued, "You check in and there's only one way to check out. Fuck, I've spent most of my life in this shithole. The All-American Industrial Motel, that's what this motherfucker is." Jerry punched his fist into the wood wall, doing his best James Dean. I started to speak but he waved me off. I turned again to run back to the dock and he called after me, trying to keep his voice down. "We're square now, right? Don't tell your old man about the thing earlier," he paused and added, "or this neither." I shook my head to indicate I'd keep it all to myself.

TWEETY NEEDS SOME CASH

Tweety Bird got my attention. "Psssssst," my mother hissed from the kitchen, standing half-hidden next to the counter and refrigerator, the feathery yellow suit as ridiculous as my dad's hairpiece. "Come here," she whispered, beckoning me with her hand to leave the dining room table and join her at the breakfast nook. I stood wearily and went to her.

I wore only a pair of boxers, having gotten a couple hours of sleep on the couch. Suddenly, I felt exposed and made certain my dinger wasn't peeking out of the fly.

"What are you doing, Mom?" She patted her sweaty forehead and dabbed under her eyes. She had to be burning up in the costume.

"Be quiet, sweetie," she said.

"You be quiet, Tweety," I responded.

My mother cut her eyes to the side, cocked her head, and held up her hand to shush me. She waited to hear something, and then relaxed a bit. "Sorry, your mother thought she heard your dad getting up."

She stood straighter and smiled, her makeup already smearing from the sweat, dark eyes even darker than normal, raccooned like a bandit. "Honey," she said, wringing her hands, "could you loan your mother some money?" Once, when I had some extra Pell Grant cash, I'd taken her to Kokomo to buy some soft-soled work shoes she needed for her grocery store job, but she'd never asked me for anything before, and I was concerned.

"Sure," I said. "You can just have it though, no loaning." I turned to retrieve my pants near the couch. She was mumbling when I returned, fishing out my wallet. "What did you say?" I asked.

She continued to whisper, afraid she'd wake my dad. "Your mother needs to buy some more material for a Porky the Pig outfit." She wiped her face again, and stood on her tiptoes to speak softly into my ear. "Your dad doesn't like me spending money on these." She pointed at her Tweety getup. It was true. With very little extra cash around, he tried to convince her that Arby's should be paying for her costume supplies. I gave her forty bucks. "Is that enough?" She exhaled in relief and swiped the money, tucked it into her purse. "Yes, sweetie. Thank you." She seemed in a hurry and planted a quick kiss on my cheek. "Your mother's got to go, hon'. There's cereal and milk, if you want some breakfast." She darted toward the door, picking up Tweety's head from a coffee table on the way. "Tell your dad I walked to work. Bye." She was out the door. I slipped around the dining table and folded back the lacy curtains. I watched her speed-walk up the street, yellow feathers pulsing in the breeze, Tweety's head tucked under her armpit. When she was nearly out of sight, the phone rang.

"Could I speak to Dan Crandell, please?" a voice said, steely and professional.

"He's not here," I lied. "Can I take a message?" It was too formal of a voice to be one of his secretive calls.

"This is the last notification of nonpayment. Please let Mr. Crandell know the electric service to this address will be cut off tonight if payment is not received at this office by close of business." The woman hung up. The steel house was in danger of losing its power, and my mother was more concerned about her Arby's crew playing dress-up.

Somewhere along the way, my parents had divvied up the bill-paying responsibilities. When he was still farming, my dad took care of those bills, and my mom was to stay on top of the household ones. But now their system was all out of whack. I heard my father stirring in the bedroom, unaware that Tweety had spent most of his paycheck on crafts, leaving us in the dark.

9

STAY AWAY FROM CARL, WY-NU-SA

For a week straight, before my summer class started, I worked on the speed and slept on the weed. In between, I drank beer out by the railroad tracks and slugged back Coca-Cola or coffee at the baler. I'd started to think this last class would be a waste of time. After all, my college professor had told us repeatedly, "Those of you who don't go on for a master's degree will most likely find work in group homes or institutions, and in effect, if you opt to do that, you should've just skipped university all together."

I left the break room and spent the rest of the night at the baler job, skipping the breaks. It was nearing midnight when my dad rolled up on the forklift, his face smoothly shaven and his toupee stiff at the edges of his hat. I hadn't asked again about Carl, or how the funeral had gone; my dad had instructed me I was not to attend, and I was relieved. The thought of seeing Carl standing next to his little girl's closed casket was more than I could take.

As if reading my mind, my dad spoke clearly but without emotion. "Carl's back. He's not gonna be able to talk about this, so just tell him hi and goodbye. Don't ask him how he's doing. You understand?" My father's words rushed over me like ice water, refreshing and brutal all at once. I pushed a green button to send a bale down the line, the white rock wool so newly spun that it gave off a burnt smell. Before I could nod in agreement, he walked to the conveyor and shut it off.

"You got a hot one," my dad said. I was taken aback for a moment, unsure of what he meant, but then I realized he was pointing at the bale, the end of it smoldering as the cardboard cap shot up in small flames. He edged me aside and yanked a fire extinguisher from the wall, sprayed the flame from more than ten feet away, killing it instantly, plumes of smoke trailing up.

"A hot coal, didn't burn up in the cupola," he said blandly, as he used a pocketknife to gouge into the bale. He twisted the blade with precision and popped the glowing rock loose. It fell to the ground, where he doused it with a short spurt of foam.

"Don't ever touch one of those. Use a knife or a pry bar to dig it out. Trucker once had to get skin grafted onto his hand after grabbing one of those sons-a-bitches without a glove."

He kicked the hunk of black toward a pile of pebble stone and sand, kept on the floor in the wool mill in case a larger fire ever broke out. The mixture could be dumped by the massive loader bucket onto a flame and knock it out in a flash. I was high and drained, speed rushing blood through the chambers of my heart as quickly as if I were running on a treadmill. He turned to look at me, and for a second I thought he'd seen the drugs in my eyes, smelled the marijuana in my clothes. Was he drinking on the job too? The smell of alcohol on him before had been strong, but perhaps it was from being around any other of the union men who reeked regularly of gin or cheap whiskey. More than anything right then, it would've done us both extra good to fess up, but the moment passed, and before I knew it my dad was back on his ride, heading out of the wool mill in a roaring blur.

It was past time to clock out when I walked toward the office he kept so orderly and clean. My plan was to try to talk with my dad, to ask about Carl and then, after we'd opened up a line of communication, ask how he himself was doing, why he'd started wearing that thing, broach the subject of the mysterious phone calls.

I edged up against the wall and crooked my head to peek inside the office. At first I didn't even see Carl, his already small body all but dwarfed by the desk. He sat numbly staring at the wall, his hands folded at his chest, his weathered lunchbox open before him. I assumed he was waiting for my father. I watched him pull a sandwich from his pail, unwrap it without even looking, put the soft white bread to his mouth, and chew weakly. Then he pulled the lunchbox toward his chest and upchucked the bite back into it. I wanted to break through the glass and hold him, to defy my father's instructions to leave him be and fumble through an awful speech about how sorry I was. But I couldn't move. Carl gingerly placed the sandwich back into his lunchbox and closed the lid.

Just then, I saw my father coming out of the office supply pantry, a woman in tow. There were just a handful of women that worked at the factory, and most of them occupied positions in the front office. She was tall and looked just like a man with a cap pulled down near her ears. My father's mouth was moving rapidly; he was talking up a storm as he and the woman approached the desk. My dad handed Carl a cup of water and a bottle of aspirin. The manly woman and my dad chatted and smiled, as Carl forced himself to swallow. Something about the way my father stood made me uneasy, as if he was excited about the future. He seemed to be bouncing on his tiptoes as he talked to her. He turned toward the window, and I thought he would see me. I started jogging away, back toward the break room.

The hurt for Carl pounded in my chest and made my stomach ache. The image of the woman and my father replayed in my head. I knew she was the person on the other end of the phone. I ran out into the parking lot without clocking out, something I knew might cost me a dock of pay, and headed quickly toward the entrance gates. I couldn't ride home with him. For certain my mother was headlong into her own form of escape, but his choice of distractions made me want to push him from the dock and onto the railroad tracks, watch as his manly body flew in all directions.

Without a ride, I started on foot for the tavern in the small town of Lagro, just a few blocks from the factory. It was pitch-dark and hot, only a sliver of moon hanging above the trees. Dogs in ramshackle houses growled and scratched at the bottoms of clattering gates. I ran harder and harder until it was difficult to inhale. Over the bridge and to the left I poured it on, as if I were about to cross a finish line. Finally, at the sidewalk leading to Fisher's, I stopped and tried to catch my breath. The music from inside rumbled the loose panes in the windows. The smacking of billiard balls made you want to chalk up a cue, bet a few bucks, and play. My dad had never said as much, but the tavern was off limits. When I was little, and my father still felt comfortable hugging his sons, my mother would bring my little sister and me to Fisher's for a treat. We'd eat French fries and sip milk out of little cartons the owner kept on hand. We'd sit in a booth and feel like big kids, and my dad would show us off to other men who happened to come inside. But our visits were only permitted during daylight hours; he never wanted us to see the same men in the condition in which I found them when I opened the heavy door, a small bell chiming, the smoke so thick it seemed as though you could nap on it like a cartoon cloud.

Sweat trickled down my spine, the waistband of my underwear wet and clammy as I walked to the bar. I knocked over a standing ashtray, and the white sand and smashed butts went everywhere. I bent and picked it up, but an old woman with an enormous belly pushed me aside and used a small brush and dustpan to clean away the mess. The stools were made of red pleather, the white tufts sprouting from slits reminded me of the rock wool, and part of me wondered if they'd actually been stuffed with it.

I ordered a Budweiser, which was all the bar served, and the bartender plopped it down in front of me with a thud, suds spilling over the rim. I threw back my head and swallowed as much in one gulp as I could. The beer was a welcome refreshment after running and I took a moment to revel in it and make believe everything was going to be OK. My dad was open, faithful, and married to my sane, craft-free mother; "lifer" wouldn't be printed on my diploma. I ordered another beer, aware that at any moment union brothers from the pool room might be rounding the bend for another drink. I'd just slugged back the second beer when Patsy and Larry burst out of the bathroom.

Patsy approached me on the invisible leash Larry pretended to hold in his hand. He wagged his butt and whimpered, acting as if he wanted petting. I ignored them and got up to go to an empty booth. But Patsy and Larry were not ones to take no for an answer. They followed me to the booth, Patsy down on all fours, really shaking his ass to imitate tail wagging. I lit a Salem and tried to act as if I knew how to smoke it. I knew I looked foolish, and it made me want to hide under the table.

Larry told his pet, "Sit boy. Sit!" Patsy acted as if he was confused, cocking his head just like a dog. I had to hand it to him, that part he had down perfectly, the tilt of the head, his scraggly beard a formidable muzzle.

Patsy turned his attention back to me, and while I should've simply given him a pat on the head, I just couldn't bring myself to do it. Instead, I drizzled some beer on top of his head. Patsy rolled onto his back and wailed, while Larry gave me a menacing look, one that meant I'd better watch it or he'd really sic his dog on me. I got up to sit back at the bar. Larry said, "Nice attitude, shithead!"

George Jones blared from the lousy speakers on the jukebox as I asked for a shot of Jack Daniels. I chased the shot with another cold draft and a shiver worked its way through my shoulders. For over an hour I sat at the bar and talked with a man named Ridley, a cattle farmer who'd allegedly drunk away all his children's inheritance. I'd known him forever; he was always stopping by the farms we rented, checking up on us. He'd met my dad shortly after the steers had been gutted by the railroad. When my parents had arrived from Terre Haute in the early 1960s, Mr. Ridley liked what he saw in my father: determination, a healthy work ethic, and the strength of a bull. The old man rented some acres to my father. While crop prices were good they both prospered, but as farming as a viable way of life disappeared, the old man slipped more and more into an oblivion of alcoholism and liver rot, and they parted ways. But Mr. Ridley still showed up at our house every few months, liquor on his breath, a jolly smile on his face. His hearty laugh was irresistible. To keep us from seeing a grandpa on the sauce, my dad would quickly escort the old man from the house, and they'd have breakfast at one of the truck stops off the highway, where semis of squalling hogs sat awaiting their awful fates while the drivers chowed down on biscuits and gravy and black coffee. Mr. Ridley was like some aged and forgotten godfather of agriculture; the ongoing visits were a way of telling my father not to give up, to keep at it. He bought me a drink and vaguely recognized me, his mind faltering. When he needed help off his stool, I was glad to prop him up on my arm. He went to the bathroom and didn't come back to the bar for a long time. When he did shuffle back over, I returned the favor and paid for his next drink, told him good-bye and left.

By 2:00 A.M. I was significantly impaired and, luckily, without a car to drive. Walking the six miles into Wabash would've been foolish, and while I could've walked back to the factory to sleep on a bench, I was afraid I'd run into my father or Carl, or the mysterious woman. It was a dilemma. Outside, the hot night air was stifling. Around the streetlights vapor roiled as moths attacked the amber light. There's a point in an Indiana summer where the haze of heat in the evening looks like the same fog as on a cold November morning. To the untrained eye, Hoosier seasons can be deceiving.

I started to walk toward the highway and was about over the bridge I'd crossed earlier when a car pulled up next to me. The brakes chirped and grinded metal on metal. I recognized the sound instantly. Jerry poked his head out the window, his generous bangs stuck to his forehead, and a glowing cigarette dangling from his slack mouth. "Get in," he said. "I'll take you home."

Jerry maneuvered his wobbly car down the black side roads toward town. The windshield was covered with the smeared guts of glowing lightning bugs and frosty moths, and he tried to use the one good wiper to clear it off. Jerry seemed quieter than normal; he hung his head some and didn't seem as edgy. I watched him in the dark car as he steered listlessly around the tight curves, the owls hooting from the thick woods, warm air blowing through the windows and flapping at his collar.

Finally, after we'd driven a few miles in silence, Jerry spoke up. "Did you hear?" I tensed. After Carl's tragedy and the way my father seemed to be willing to burn down his life to determine if he was indeed alive, I'd begun to assume all news was bad.

"No, what?" I asked, Jerry already rolling a doobie with one hand while steering poorly with the other. I reached over and took the wheel; after killing the calf, I wanted to be extra careful.

Jerry licked the paper and rolled the joint against his dirty pant leg; resulting in a slightly tan doobie, grungy and lumpy. He lit the joint and slapped his lighter shut, puffed and held his breath, handed the marijuana to me. I let loose of the steering wheel as Jerry took over. He sniffed through his nose forcefully, making a gooselike sound. He did it all the time, and the honk was always startling. If you were in public with him and he snorted like this, bystanders would turn and gawk as if viewing a performer in a sideshow.

"They found asbestos in the old motel," he said. "From when they used to make tile with it. We all gotta get tested. They're gonna start removal this week. I saw the outfits those guys wear. Look like space aliens." Jerry put on the brakes at the dirt entrance to a place called Hanging Rock, a limestone overhang that plunges toward the Wabash River, a remnant of a huge reef dating back to the existence of the Silurian seas more than 400 million years ago. It's also the birthplace of a legend about a Miami Indian maiden named Wy-nu-sa. According to lore, two braves were in love with her and challenged one another to a duel on top of the rock. They fought, brandishing tomahawks and stone knives, until one pushed the other over the edge to his death. The exhausted brave walked toward Wy-nu-sa and began to take her into his sweaty arms, but she was heartbroken, and screamed that he'd killed her true love. She ran and jumped off Hanging Rock herself so that she could be with her soul mate forever in the Happy Hunting Ground.

Bleary-eyed Jerry finally looked directly at me. He had a grin on his face, a sign the pot was working on him. "Looks like we're gonna have us some E.T. martian motherfuckers working at the old motel for a while, Crandell." He burst out giggling and honking. Walking up the dark trail to Hanging Rock, we held our stomachs from laughing. Our feet cracked twigs and threw dirt. When we reached the top, Jerry said, suddenly serious, "You think that pretty maiden really leaped off this son-of-a-bitch?" We looked at one another and burst out laughing once again, the Wabashiki River below us gurgling, the white dalles unseen in the pitch-dark night. It was right then, with Jerry hunched over, his childish snickering stealing all his breath, that we became friends.

Jerry confessed, more solemn now, "I'm sorry I've gotten you into this." He held up the joint and pointed to it. He hugged me briefly and patted me on the back, sniffled. All my life he'd been frightening, too wild and dangerous for me to be left alone with him as a child, but now, Jerry filled a void. How we didn't plunge to our deaths that night, like the Indian brave and Wy-nu-sa, was as much a mystery to me as my father's behavior. We sat on a log and passed the joint back and forth. It was a bit cooler atop the rock, the treetops swaying gently.

In my college speech class a year before, one of the students had given a report on asbestos, how it was one of industry's hidden plagues, something that their law departments calculated the cost of using top-secret formulas. For a moment, I had a vision of Wy-nu-sa punching a Texas Instruments calculator, tallying up numbers as long as my arm, but a heaviness fell onto my shoulder and brought me out of the dream. Jerry was out cold, his head like a child's slipping down onto my chest. I imagined the hyaline river below us, and wondered if any of the asbestos had ever ridden its current.

GARLIC AND BROWNIES

I smelled the garlic so strongly I thought a strand was around my neck. In the heat, I believed I might be dining in a real Italian kitchen. My body was numb, and the left side of my face felt perforated, hot and sticky and tingly. I opened one eye and saw only a grillwork of some sort, a black vent. My legs were asleep and I had to urinate so badly my whole midsection was on fire. Drool was dried to my open mouth, and I realized I was lying flat on my stomach, head turned to the side. The vent took shape through my eye, gluey with sleep. It was the bottom of the refrigerator, and the piercing feeling on my left cheek was the Berber carpet in our kitchen. Under my chest I felt a slimy hunk of something; it squished when I made any movement at all.

I tried to recall getting home. I pictured Jerry and me fiddling dangerously on the edge of Hanging Rock, making wide hand motions, indicating our great ideas and intricate philosophical positions. Two drunken stoners thinking they'd figured out the cloaked mysteries of the known world.

I rolled over onto my side and started to make out a figure standing over me. It had on a furry black suit, a large white oval in the center, and the tail curled down to the floor, tickling my bare thigh. The figure above me held the head of a large mammal tucked under its arm. My mother's face appeared clearly in one blink, blurry the next. She was in her Arby's Sylvester the Cat costume. I could hear her saying something, pointing down at my bare chest.

"Baby, what is that?" She pointed again, as I tried to dip my head enough to get a gander. I struggled again and again as her face scrunched up into a disgusted expression, not at her son but at whatever was stuck to his pale chest. The odor of garlic became stronger, wafted up in my face.

Sylvester backed up and turned to put her head on the table, her pear-shaped body so sad and vulnerable in that outfit. She pulled a chair over next to me and I propped myself up on it. The item remained fastened to my chest, smashed into the paltry hair, my nipples greasy. "Dougie, what is that thing?" A fleeting image of me digging through the freezer blipped into my mind.

I'd come home hungry and scrounged around the kitchen in the dark, trying to make certain I didn't wake anyone. The cookie jar held only crumbs of graham crackers, and the bread bin was empty. A drunken inspection of the crisper drawers only produced a bag of shrinking mini-carrots and rubbery celery. I had the munchies and needed something substantial, something to sleep on. Finally, I'd pawed at the freezer door and found a loaf of frozen garlic bread. It should have gone in the oven or microwave to defrost, but I couldn't wait. What did I do? My brain struggled to assemble the pieces from the night before. Did I try and nuke it? Was the oven involved? No, I finally realized, I'd tucked it under my body to warm it up, not wanting to mess with the burdensome twentieth-century contraptions made for such a task. The frozen loaf felt cool on my body, and I fell asleep on top of it, keeping it safe like a hen protecting its chick.

I sat in the chair and peeled the bread from my chest. My mother couldn't look away, as if staring with disgust at something dead on the side of the road. "Gross," she said, her broad nose turned up, as she went to the sink. I ran through in my sluggish brain what I could tell her, but it didn't matter. She'd never admit to herself that I was using drugs or drinking or passing out on the hot floor of the steel house. She returned to where I sat, a steaming kitchen towel in her hand. She began wiping my chest clean, a motion that made me sick to my stomach. I knew I was preparing to vomit, and I stood up quickly from the chair and rushed to the bathroom. For her sake, I turned on the water.

. . .

Right around the time the basketball court was constructed I had my soul saved. It was at a Friends Quaker Church. The youth pastor there was a weight lifter who reminded me of Lou Ferrigno. He prayed over me and asked if I'd accept Jesus into my heart. I said yes, partly because I wanted to, but also because I was afraid he could snap me in two if I went with the devil. He had us sign contracts in which we pledged we'd remain drug-free. That night my dad picked me up from the church. In the truck he asked, "What's that you got there?" speaking from one side of his mouth, a newly lit cigarette dangling from the other.

"Nothing. Just a pledge." I hoped he'd leave it at that, but he reached for the paper and read it under the passing streetlights on our way through the outskirts of town, heading toward our failing farm.

He handed it back to me as he rolled down the window to let the smoke out. He bent to tap ashes into the cuff of his jeans, a habit I'd started to understand was meant to keep a dry field from igniting.

"That's good, son," he commented, handing the pledge back to me. "Something like that can help keep you focused." He steered the truck onto the potholed one-lane road that led to the farm. It was dark outside; only the lights of different farms twinkled in the distance. I wanted to tell him more, ask questions about why he didn't believe, reveal myself, but when the truck stopped in front of the house the moment was over. "I got to pull a double shift tonight, son. You get your sleep." He reached over my lap to open my door, and I was tempted to hug him as hard as I could. I stepped out of the truck and he yanked the door shut. I watched as he backed up and drove quickly out of sight.

. . .

Since the Incredible Hulk at church had saved me in junior high, I hadn't been any trouble to my parents. The anti-drug pledge I'd signed had worked up until college, and I suppose my mother had gotten accustomed to thinking of me as squeaky clean. She had good reason, too. Once, when I was in tenth grade, I was invited to a campfire party at the Mississinewa Reservoir. Someone told me it was BYO—bring your own—which I assumed meant snacks and drinks. On the evening of the event, I dressed in my pleated pants and matching suspenders and a dress shirt with an oval collar and fake gold stay with chain. I wore a thin, shiny necktie of pink, yellow, and blue pastels. I was decked out. In a mixing bowl I emptied a Betty Crocker brownie mix and added eggs and oil, beat them together, and carefully greased a nine-by-eleven-inch pan. I retrieved a cooler from the garage and packed the brownies, covered three times in Saran Wrap, into the bottom, along with a gallon jug of chocolate milk.

I was proud to be driving to one of my first parties. Along the way I listened to REO Speedwagon and doused my shirtfront with my brother's cologne. My hair was feathered on top, but permed in the back, giving it two distinct textures. At the reservoir, kids hauled coolers like mine to the bonfire, boom boxes on their shoulders and strange suede pouches slung across their torsos, filled, I'd find out later, with Jack Daniels and grape Kool-Aid. Once we were all seated next to the fire, someone said, "Hey Crandell, did you think this was one of your youth group parties? What's with the clothes?" A few people laughed, and I tried a witty comeback that flopped immediately. As kids began slugging back drinks from the leather pouches, purple rings around their mouths, I felt stupid to have brought the brownies and milk. Luckily, since few people were talking to me, I was able to slip away and drive back toward home.

Hungry for a snack in the car, I reached to open the cooler. My suspenders latched onto the gear shift and pulled the engine into neutral, which in turn freaked me out to the point of slamming on the brakes. I mildly crashed into a fence, and could've gotten out eventually, but someone from one of the nearby houses called the sheriff. Two deputies drove up, sirens blaring, probably expecting to find another drunk kid dead on the scene. Instead, they found a well-groomed dork trying to pull sod from the car's grill. They spotted the cooler and ordered me to open it. They shined their flashlights inside and looked confused. "What is that?" one asked. I told them I'd made brownies and that the jug was chocolate milk. Disbelieving, they opened the milk jug and sniffed as I told them I was on my way home because the party out at the reservoir was not what I'd assumed it was. One of the deputies, a man in his early fifties, became choked up. "Son," he said, with emotion thick in his throat, "you just made my whole year." With that, he and the other deputy pushed the car from the ditch and I was on my way, a Betty Crocker nerd to my peers, a sign of generational hope to the gentle officers. Later, I'd find out the party was busted and raided. I heard people saying they'd get the person who'd tipped off the fuzz.

. . .

Now, though, I yakked repeatedly into the commode, then finally washed my face and brushed my teeth. I reached for a hand towel and nearly screamed when my hand felt the stiff hair of my dad's toupee. "Shit," I said, catching my breath. I stumbled out of the bathroom and into the living room, where I flopped down on the couch. No air conditioning. On top of the television was a sleigh made from the breastbone of a turkey ten years before. My mother had fashioned it into Santa's ride by boiling it until all the fat and meat were removed, then air-drying the bone in the sun until it turned white. She brushed some glue onto the sleigh and sprinkled some of the silver glitter she loved so much over it. After attaching a plastic team of reindeer, Rudolph in his guiding position, she stuck a Weeble outfitted in a tiny Santa suit she'd fashioned out of cotton balls and a red handkerchief into the breastbone sleigh. We were all amazed, and told her so. She reveled in the praise, and kept the sleigh on top of the TV from then on. I stared at it as I lay hungover and queasy on the stifling couch. I started to drift back to sleep when my mother came walking through the house again, about to head out the door to Arby's.

"You better get going, honey," she said, her tail almost catching in the door. Nothing registered. Going where? I sat up and felt as if molten rock had set up in my rear; I was a Weeble myself, wobbling, but not quite falling down.

"You know, your class at the college. Today's your first day, remember?" How she'd found the time and energy to remember was not something I could decipher. She worked long hours at the fast food joint and kept the house while my dad and I rarely landed there at all. She smiled weakly in my direction and closed the screen door. The car started up and I watched through the picture window as she backed out the drive and over the curb, the car rocking back and forth when she put it in forward and drove over the curb again. As she pulled away, her Sylvester tail hung out the door, just clearing the burning-hot pavement as she drove the posted speed limit of 15 miles per hour away from the steel house. I got up and went to my stash, a baggy of speed I'd hid under the sink. The drive from Wabash to Muncie would take a little over an hour, and I needed to be alert. I popped two pills and reached for the fridge, pulled out a jug of milk and took a swig.

There was a knock on the door just as I made myself swallow. I walked into the living room and looked toward the screen, a few flies buzzing in the center. I hadn't seen much of any of my siblings that summer, so I was bewildered to see my two brothers, Derrick and Darren, standing on the front porch, looking like they had a present to deliver.

I hadn't given much thought to how I was going to drive back and forth from the factory in Lagro to school in Muncie, but, like always, my brothers came through for me. Their plan was to loan me Derrick's black Monte Carlo for the summer. In turn, Darren would loan Derrick something to drive. Both of my brothers had married and were trying to start lives of their own, penny-strapped and working long hours themselves—Derrick as a truck driver and Darren for an electrical supply company. Even so, they'd found the time to think of me. It was a sacrifice that matched the others they'd made for me during my years in college. They'd bought me groceries, sent money for gas bills, and shipped care packages with razors, boxes of cereal, and twenty-dollar bills tucked inside the pockets of new shirts. My brothers got me through college, and sometimes I wonder if they'd always known the only way I was going to survive in the world was if I had a piece of paper that said I could.

PSYCH! IT'S SEX ED

Instead of making me feel less sick, the chilly central air conditioning in the classroom gave my skin an icy clam, raising goose bumps along my arms and neck. The professor, a skinny man with pale hair and wide-set eyes the color of sandpaper, wore a loose-fitting pair of khakis and flip-flops, his short-sleeved shirt untucked and wrinkled, a real beach bum prof.

There were more empty seats than full, about fifteen students in all, and most of them summer-tuition brats, kids whose parents forked over the cash for their short semester on campus so they didn't have to hassle with a job. The same kids who had their own cars to drive to class instead of having to walk, the ones I'd felt completely unconnected to for four years.

I knew one student in the class, a senior with just a few credit hours left to graduate as well. His name was Richard, and he lived in Yorktown, less than twenty minutes away. We'd met while working at a Chinese restaurant the previous fall. He was very overweight and sported terribly large eyeglasses. His face was pocked with acne scars, and he never tied his shoes. Like me, he made tuition on summer jobs, work-study, and student loans. Richard spotted me and nodded his head imperceptibly. He'd grown a shabby, light-colored beard since I'd last seen him that created a peachy softness from under his neck almost up to his eye sockets.

The professor wrote the name of the class on the board, his pinky ring scraping the slate. Once he finished and stepped away from the board, it read: Psychology of Sexual Behavior! He walked slowly toward his desk and sat down on the edge, folded his hands under his chin as if in prayer. "What is sex?" he asked, a causal, sincere look on his tan face, forehead knitted into a specific thought, eyebrows cinched. No one answered. The few girls in the class popped gum and giggled. One, a young woman sitting away from the others, finally said, "It depends."

"On what?" the professor asked, leaning forward.

"On if you're in love." She sat with perfect posture in a Fellowship of Christian Athletes sweatshirt, ready to defend all that was matrimonial about sexual reproduction. I felt sorry for her. She was going to take a beating.

A frat guy with his hat on backwards and a pair of red Chuck Taylors laced tight chimed in. "Sex is fucking. Plain and simple. It's just no one wants to admit it."

The young woman tried to appear calm, unshaken. She shook her head. "No. That may be what you think, but sex is about love and commitment." She took out her notebook and flipped to a blank page, clicking an ink pen in and out, over and over.

"Well, you're both right," said the diplomatic professor, his hands now shoved into his pockets, the material bulging with clenched fists.

"The thing is, we've all got different notions of what sex and love are." He walked toward a projector atop a rolling stand. "To better illustrate this point, we're going to watch a film that will make many of you uncomfortable. Remember, this is an elective course for your completion of an undergrad in psychology. If you find yourself having difficulty with the subject matter of this film, it will be a good barometer of how the next five weeks will be for you. Anyone who wants to leave may do so at any time. If you choose to, see your advisor and they'll be able to help you quickly choose another elective to fulfill your course requirements." He walked to the doorway, his flip-flops patting dully, and dimmed the lights.

The film wasted no time. A woman in the throes of birth was pushing hard, sweating profusely on her thighs as a hairy baby's head crowned from an equally hairy area. With one slobbery thrust the child was ushered into the world—mucous, blood, and all. He screamed in a high pitch, little gums as vacant as Henry's at the factory. The narrator went on to offer up the many configurations and purposes humankind has forged for sex: commerce, proliferation, pleasure, love, even torture. For the next ten minutes the screen was filled with shots of couples kissing, dancing, and engaging in soft-core sex. Then, without warning, the film switched into shock mode. An elderly couple in their eighties struggled to achieve penetration near a lake then engaged in a bare-naked interview; the topic: their life-long adventures together as unmarried sexual partners. They talked about stubborn ejaculation, their use of sex toys, and how old age had made copulation even more challenging. They laughed in their withered bodies, his breasts as saggy and ample as hers. When they began hotly kissing again, sometimes missing each other's mouths, weak, mottled hands shaking, the film faded into another scene. Suddenly, a man was giving oral sex to another man in the backseat of a car. The narrator said, "No topic in America's collective sexual consciousness is more taboo and controversial than homosexuality." Many of the students made audible sounds of disgust, and two of the frat guys left. The film ended and the lights flicked back on. The professor started another diatribe about how the next five weeks would challenge our sense of right and wrong, our values and conventions, our religious beliefs. "Now's the time to make the decision. I just wanted you all to know what you're in for here." The class turned toward a sound at the back of the room. The young woman who'd spoken up earlier, asserting that sex was the equivalent of love, was trying to hold back tears as she gathered her denim backpack and leather purse. Without a word, she scampered from the room sniffling.

"Anybody else?" The professor scanned the room. "There's nothing wrong with deciding this class isn't for you, but do it now, not later when you feel misled and want to file a complaint." About twelve students remained, and for the remainder of the class the professor went over when and how the tests would be administered and handed out a syllabus. To my surprise, the class went by quickly, and before I knew it I was on my way back to the bright, blazing parking lot.

On the drive back I left the windows down, the humid wind blowing, almost taking my syllabus right out of the car. At a desolate four-way stop I lit a joint and smoked it with gusto. It took the edge off, even though I knew I would need something else to bring me back into work mode. Sitting motionless on the shoulder of the road, I watched the flawless blue sky as birds skittered from tree to telephone wire. Perched in a row, they appeared as one, a bracelet of dark, shivering jewels. I was stoned and dumb, and when the image of Carl puking into his lunch bucket surfaced, I believed I saw its beauty. Nothing is more stupid or sad than a stoner thinking he's being deep.

12

THE UNITED BOYS' CHEERLEADING UNION

When I was sixteen I wanted to get my father's attention. We were from two very different generations, true, and learning to be a man in the 1950s was useless to me in the 1980s, but there was something else that made us different too. I craved the opportunity to examine my emotions, to pinpoint why I was feeling a certain way, while my father viewed manhood as a silent journey, one that should be stoic and absent of weakness. He believed that any emotion other than anger and disappointment was feminine, and it was that belief that caused in me the desire to hurt him.

It was 1984, and my jump shot, while awkward and fraught with technical imperfections, was consistent and quick. Since my dad and I had buried the time capsule together three years earlier, I'd practiced on the court for hours on end, dribbling around chairs strategically placed to imitate defensive players. My dad had sent me to basketball camps and made it to most of my games from seventh to tenth grade. With the factory and the failing farm at his back, it was amazing he had any time at all, but my playing the sport was a source of pride for him—something I decided to use against him.

By the time I reached puberty, my dad had stopped showing any physical affection toward me, and his words were just as spare as always. He was distant and cold, and I quit playing basketball just to make him feel something. Like a junkie wielding a knife, I cut him deep just to see how he would react. He didn't speak to me for a couple months after I announced I wouldn't play anymore, but I wanted to make it worse, drive the point home. Joining the cheerleading squad seemed to be just the right move.

Southwood High School hadn't had male cheerleaders in all its history, so it took extra effort and spite to convince the athletic department to permit it. Myself, along with several other guys with nothing else to do, pitched the idea and found ourselves shocked when ushered into the art room to be fitted with tight T-shirts and wristbands the same colors as the girls' pompoms.

Basketball fans in Indiana, whether of high school or college teams, are rabid. Families plan outings around the games; elderly grandparents are gurneyed in from their nursing homes to watch Joey play point guard before a home-court crowd decked out in all manner of team-spirit paraphernalia. Local AM radio stations deliver live broadcasts that equal anything on primetime cable networks. Farmers take breaks from harvesting corn and soybeans just to wander into a packed gymnasium to watch a game they've got no kids playing in, their dusty overalls smeared with axle grease, their windburnt faces lighting up at the possibility of a breakaway layup while munching on buttery popcorn from the concession stand.

After suiting up the week before in the cheerleader outfit, which included red pants, I'd started to think I'd made a mistake. I was certain I had when we began practicing cheers for the upcoming game. No matter how much I tried to use a deep voice, I sounded like a pre-teen girl as I chanted "Let's Get a Little Bit Rowdy!" And then there was "You Ain't Seen Nothin' Yet," with its alluring, hip-rolling melody, thumbs hitching a ride along with the beat. It was more than I'd counted on, and even I was embarrassed to watch my male cohorts perform.

The night of the big game arrived, and I told myself the embarrassment was worth it. If I was going to cut my father, this would be it, his former basketball-playing son now a cheerleader. Sure, he wouldn't be in attendance because of overtime, and he didn't even know I'd signed up to cheer, but it was a small town, and I knew word would get to him somehow. In the locker room I looked in the mirror. My pants were grossly too tight, and because my lips were chapped I'd applied Vaseline, which only added to their raw redness and made it look like I was wearing lipstick. I went to the sink and tried to wipe my mouth off, but it only made it worse. The gymnastics coach, who was also the mentor of the cheerleading squad, knocked on the door and called us out. "Come on, boys, it's time to take the floor." The red pants rubbed at my thighs as I left the locker room.

Out on the gym floor, the crowd was immense, a sea of rollicking fans shouting and waving banners, little kids on tops of shoulders, music from the band blaring. I couldn't remember any of the words to the cheers, and when I recognized a part where the boys were to follow the girls' lead, strut our stuff, hips a-go-go, I wasn't able to get in synch. Every time I thought I'd gotten the pelvic thrust going in the right direction, I was already behind again. The result was something akin to a toy poodle distracted by a live audience as it tries in vain to perform a hula-hoop act. The tight pants didn't help.

Finally, our performance was over and we exited the floor. As I was about to make a full-blown sprint into the safety of the locker room, I noticed a gang of factory men leaning against the wall, most of whom were well aware that I was Dan Crandell's son. I dipped my head, and one of the men whistled a catcall; it was Jerry. They were drunk on gin and smoking even though it was prohibited in the gym.

I dashed into the locker room and stripped off the red pants for the comfort of a pair of Levi's.

For a week after my cheerleading debut, I limped from a pulled muscle in my groin and truly feared I'd given myself a hernia or ruptured a vital reproductive organ. I'd cheer for a few more home games, and that would be it. A few years later, when I went to work at the factory, a guy who worked the midnight shift gave me a double-take as he clocked in. He said, "Hey weren't you a cheerleader for Southwood?"

My father never responded in any way, and for years we struggled to find a line of communication after I'd effectively severed the one topic we seemed to come together around, basketball. My plan had backfired. That's the problem with revenge; the perpetrator always ends up the victim, one way or another.

PART II

July 1990

"We can now see the factory as a web of social inter-relationships with certain areas of tension which cause those situated at such points to become sick."

—J. A. C. BROWN, *Human Relations in the Factory*

ASBESTOS SNOW GLOBE

The shift schedule had me working back on the other side of the factory, away from the wool mill I'd come to find comfort and belonging in, with its repetitive processes, deafening furnaces, and scent of burning wool like that of autumn leaves on fire. As I clocked in I spotted Henry. He peered at the week's schedule, which was pinned to a corkboard and covered with a hinged Plexiglas case to keep the men from tampering with the penciled-in job assignments.

"Looks like you're leaving me, son." He studied the job postings more closely, said without looking at me, "Better watch it over there on that side. There's something tearing open whole skids of boxes. Like a lunatic devil or something. They say you can feel spots of real cold air. That's spooks for sure." He took the first bite off a Honey Bun, the wrapper perfectly folded down to keep his dirty hands from touching its sticky glaze. Henry's set of teeth was plunked down in his shirt pocket, the outline of them visible through his gauzy pocket-T. The dentures hurt him when he chewed, and he preferred to wear them for cosmetic purposes only. He gummed another bite of his treat and meticulously rolled down the wrapper.

Once, when we were all sitting on the dock, basking in the setting sun during the last break of the evening, the breeze easing over our sweat-drenched clothes, another college kid teased Henry about his nickname.

"MF, were you really someone's bitch at Pendleton?" The kid grinned while shoving a Ho Ho into his mouth. Henry didn't respond, his teeth in his pocket, head down, whistling air across the top of a hot cup of coffee from his thermos. The kid wouldn't stop though and said with a pie-hole of blackness, cream filling on his lips, "Well, were ya? Did you let someone do that to you?" Henry stood and sipped from the silver cup, his black eyes moist. He took a step away from the dock, preparing to leave. His hands shook. He paused and reflected, his dark eyes scanning the fading sunset. The kid waited for a response while the rest of us sat silently, cowards who neither wanted to hear the answer nor were able to admit that we'd had the same, morbid thought.

Henry gripped the thermos cup tightly and sat back down, crossing his legs Indian style, which I was surprised he could manage. He placed his cup carefully on the cement and cleared his throat. He ran his hand through his dyed-black hair, the scabs on his knuckles from the hot furnace catching some strands, while all of us listened intently for his response. Finally, after he'd rubbed his eyes with the butts of his palms, Henry pursed his empty mouth and offered up an answer. He looked directly at the kid and said, "What would you do if someone had a knife to your throat and said 'Shit on my dick or blood on my blade'?"

The kid stopped chewing and slowly shrugged his shoulders. Henry looked around the group and changed the subject. "Come on now, we've got plant clean-up tour tonight. Let's get busy." From down the railroad tracks, a train just passing by the town of Huntington tooted its horn then blew it three times in a row, a sound I'd forever associate with Henry, its lonely call so distinct and soothing, a sign we can outlive what we once were, bypass those old notions of ourselves and rise to the surface a new being. I stood and brushed off my pants, bent down and picked up Henry's thermos. I didn't want anyone to call him MF ever again.

As I walked beside Henry now, back into the belly of the factory, speed rushing through me, he bumped me at the arm and pointed. "Look there, son. They got those men suited up to remove that 'bestos." The men worked inside a tent that reminded me of the John Travolta movie *The Boy in the Plastic Bubble*. Inside the tent a vacuum device sputtered and took hold, as one of the men used a hose to clean away the dust and rock wool and old pigeon feathers of a hundred years, accumulated hour by hour, shift by shift, from one union contract to another.

It takes just one little fiber of microscopic size to start asbestosis. The factory had been manufacturing at least a dozen different insulation products dating back to the 1930s and 1940s, before much was known about how harmful exposure to the deadly fibers could be. Smoking brings the disease on more rapidly, and the factory was full of smokers. The place had thousands of pipes and electrical conduits crisscrossing one another above our heads, each one holding the dust and filaments of thirty years of production, every inch conceivably contaminated with asbestos. As I watched the men work in their bubble, I couldn't help thinking of my father. By that time, he'd worked in the factory for over twenty years, pulling double and triple shifts over and over.

Henry took me by the arm and urged me to follow him. "Let's get outta here, son. That shit must be bad stuff if they get all dressed up like that." I followed, both of us looking over our shoulders at the men moving in slow motion, so carefully they seemed to be walking on the moon in zero gravity. I would only get to work with Henry again one more time, late in the summer, but I didn't know that then. All I knew for certain was that his touch, the concern in his voice, and the way he didn't let go of my arm until we got into the wool mill, seemed more like weightless love to me than mere union-brother duty. I think of that walk often, at nights mostly, when I hear a train, or see an old man walking with pride down the street. It's a memory I've never lost, one that I feel so fortunate to have; me and the man they called a bad name, walking like a married couple toward the snowy mill, the wool falling like soft flakes all around us. It would make a good scene in a snow globe; shake it up and watch the white particles swarm around a former prison inmate and a stoner college kid. See if, when it all settles, they turn into something different, transcend their lots, check out of the motel.

14

STORMING THE DESERT

It was rare to be sitting at the kitchen table with my father. As the summer passed he'd become even more withdrawn, his toupee less and less cared for. The conditioner that smelled like shoe polish wasn't worked through the hairpiece with care on a daily basis, and when it was put to rest at night, it might just as easily turn up on the top of the toilet tank as on the wire ball with stem that was supposed to let it breathe for eight hours to keep the odor from sweat to a minimum.

We drank black coffee and mumbled questions and answers to one another under the blaring TV about which shift we'd pulled, what overtime was available. The electricity was still on; my mother had avoided the cutoff somehow.

It looked like the country was going to end up in a war after all. Kuwait had been invaded and speculation was rampant. A news anchor seated in a mauve studio interviewed another reporter stationed in a sandy and windblown top-secret location. Wearing fatigues and a large helmet, the man on the scene gave updates about the diplomatic breakdowns to date. My dad lit a cigarette and blew smoke away from me. My mother had to report early at Arby's.

As the news report ended, my dad stood and walked to the set, switched it off. He said, "How many classes you got yet?" I told him just the one.

"When's it over?"

"Five weeks, or so."

"You best see about taking more." He pointed to the TV set. "Hell knows what that mess will turn into." The short show of concern receded into a flash of furrowed brow. He went into the bathroom. From the table where I sat chewing on a burnt Pop-Tart, I heard water flood the basin and the rapid rinsing of his old razor: thwack, stroke, thwack, stroke, again and again. As a kid I'd watched him shave a thousand times, his patience more steady then, willing to entertain a chubby five-year-old whose main interest was watching his father use manly care to keep his face the smooth and good-smelling surface I loved to kiss and pat when I sat on his lap.

The steel house was hotter than ever, the stagnant air inside forcing me to the porch. My bare feet padded across the cement toward the single lawn chair that sat next to a wobbly table covered in water rings. I sat my coffee down and dug my fingers into the pocket of my jeans, felt the joint there and calculated in my head the time my father still required in the bathroom. The daily combination of weed and speed was taking its toll on me. Add in the booze and too little rest, and it was difficult to imagine I would pass the last college course I needed for graduation.

Quickly, I lit the joint and sucked in, held the smoke in my lungs. As fast as I could, I toked and toked until my eyes watered and my thoughts quieted. I slugged back the rest of the coffee and got up from the lawn chair. Birds tweeted along the roofline of the sagging garage, their white droppings appearing as splotches of rare art on the green shingles. I took the roach and placed it under a clay pot of dried-up flowers near the garage door. If I needed it later, I could put it together with the others I'd stashed under other pots, along ledges, and behind the insulation in the garage. I could roll a whole doobie out of the leftovers. A few cars passed by on the road out front, and something hummed above my head. A gigantic wasp hive crawled with workers, in and out of the perfect holes, marching with purpose from one sector to another. I threw my head back further and inspected the hive as I swatted mosquitoes near my shins, the dry grass like scouring pads under my feet. Wasps passed each other in perfect isolation, working diligently at their individual tasks but somehow managing to forge a whole. Stoned, I decided once again I'd found a great analogy for the factory. I gazed up and nodded in solidarity toward the hive, pleased with myself.

With my head nearly parallel to the sky, I didn't see the wasp slip down the back of my T-shirt. At first I didn't feel the sting. When I did I started to howl and dance, flapping my arms behind me like chicken wings as I tried in vain to rid the middle of my back of the stinger. I'd twirled around in a circle several times when, as if on a carousel, I saw first at one rotation, then another, my father standing at the edge of the sidewalk staring at me in bewilderment.

I slowed myself down until I finally stopped completely and faced him. There are moments when a son knows his father's expectations haven't been met, when he can physically feel the disappointment. I pointed up to indicate the hive, but my father had already walked to the old car and climbed in. He popped his head out the window as he put the car in reverse, right arm swung over the bench seat, ready to back out. He said, "They called you in early. Foreman phoned. I told him you'd be there." With that he shot out of the driveway and took off, the jalopy jerking and sputtering in protest as he backfired down the street and onto the highway toward the factory.

I stood embarrassed under the hive, the sting on my back on fire. I'd not slept more than five hours in three days, and I was exhausted.

I needed to be at the factory for a sixteener in less than two hours. I went inside, fixed a box of macaroni and cheese and ate it all right out of the saucepan, gobbled up a peanut butter sandwich and washed it down with an ice-cold Coke. Then I showered, got dressed, and popped some pills. Wired and edgy, I got into the car Derrick had loaned me and started toward the factory earlier than needed, afraid I'd accidentally fall asleep if I read or watched television, even with the speed coursing through my veins.

Out on the hot pavement, I checked the rearview mirror to make sure no cops were on my trail. Still hungry, I stopped at a convenience store and picked up a king-sized Snickers and another Coke. I lumbered across the lot toward the car and looked up at the rough sound of a motorcycle chugging along slowly on the street. The rider looked familiar; he didn't wear a helmet, and when he stopped at the light, I realized it was my brother Derrick. I was stunned. So I'd have his car to drive back and forth to Muncie for my class and into Lagro for the factory work, he'd borrowed Darren's old motorcycle. Derrick was a horrible driver on two wheels. With legs like tree trunks, he struggled to keep the small bike balanced while waiting for the light to turn. And then, big fat drops of summer rain began to smack his back and head. Finally he eased the motorcycle through the intersection, hair now sopping wet, his full beard dripping rain. I stood there and watched him disappear over the swell in the road, his hunched figure bearing down against the storm.

THE SAINTLY CHURCH OF MIDLIFE CRISIS

Jesuit missionaries traveling from Montreal on their way to the outpost of Vincennes, Indiana, stopped in Lagro in about 1800. Nearly forty years later, the Wabash and Erie Canals would open up, and the tiny town would become a central shipping point for wheat and corn, drawn along the waters by docile mares steadily trooping up and down the muddy banks. Irish-Catholic families traveled from the east and settled in Lagro and the surrounding county. In 1838 Thomas Fitzgibbon donated two lots, where a thirty-by-forty-foot frame building was erected and named St. Patrick's Church. It housed several groups with names like the Rosary Society, the Total Abstinence Society, and the Young Ladies' Sodality group, which performed charitable work for the poor and needy immigrants settling in the area.

The church is beautiful, ornate in trim yet simple in design. A welcoming sidewalk leads to heavy doors under a small portico. I'd gotten an early start and still had an hour before I had to clock in at the factory. I drove past the church, turned around in a potholed lane, and cruised back by, finally stopping at the curb. I got out and walked toward the towering church. The rain had stopped and now the smell of the midsummer shower steamed from the hot street and made everything drip, silver and syncopated. It would do nothing to help the drought, but it was beautiful. I walked past the church first, and then back by again, looking it over. I hadn't been inside a church for a few years, but I had never stopped praying or reading the Bible, even if I sometimes preferred the scariest parts, Job and Revelation. Near the steps a little girl was watching me suspiciously, her small forehead crinkled against the blaring sun. She was about ten, tiny kneecaps scabbed, a shiny little bobbed haircut framing her round face. I'd seen her near town before; she had a learning disability, and each time I'd seen her she struggled to peddle her bike, which still had training wheels on it, over the crumbled sidewalks. Now she hopped on the bike and slowly clambered away from me.

I wasn't sure what I wanted from the church, pacing casually past a few more times before climbing back into the car and speeding away, over the bridge and down Main Street to the factory. Just before I turned in past the guard shack, I caught a glimpse of my father near the back of the plant, where an elaborate maze of chutes, augers, and elevators with rusty catwalks hung suspended in the air like an abstract sculpture. He was alone, leaning against the wall. As I slowed down, I saw him take a long swig from a bottle. He wiped his mouth and shoved the bottle under an old bench. I put my hand on the door handle and unlatched it, the car idling, still in gear. In less than thirty seconds I could run to him and end it all, hug him tight and confess my own troubles, confront him about his. I shoved the car in park and opened the door wider, put my foot out. But a semi's brakes hissed near the dock and made my dad look up. I closed the door and gunned the car so he wouldn't see me and parked far away from the entrance. Several vans from the asbestos removal company sat nearby, backdoors flung open, an assortment of gear dangling from hooks: helmets, puffy suits, and chrome gas masks. I turned off the engine and felt hopeless. I could start the car back up and drive away, steal my brother's Monte Carlo and head out on the highway toward someplace, any place other than Lagro, Indiana, but instead I stepped out of the car and started the trek toward the time clock. I needed the money, but I was scared to leave, too, afraid I wouldn't make it on my own. The factory percolated in front of me, smoke and exhaust spewing into the air, creating elongated clouds, dun and gray. The thought of another double shift was enough to make me want to sprint back to the church in town and hide beneath a pew, listen for a benediction that might save me, my father, and all the other union men. Maybe I would end up a lifer after all.

DORIS! TEAM #1!

The transfer from Henry's wool mill back to the production line was tough. The hours seemed longer, and sneaking outside to the railroad tracks was risky. Plus, I was actually afraid to be around the warehouse by myself. More and more cartons of torn-up tile kept appearing, and no one knew why. Stories of disturbed ghosts were rampant. Some said they were the souls of the men who'd died violent deaths in the plant in the 1940s, unsettled and unwilling to go into the afterlife, trapped for eternity in the factory. Rumors of missing box cutters and tales of hovering plasmatic figures filled the break room.

After clocking in I looked up every time I heard a forklift go by, hoping to see my father so I could gauge his state of mind. But if it was him, I never got a real good look; whoever it was blew by so fast they could've been cited by management for violating the speed limit.

Just before dinnertime, the clock on the wall ticked slowly toward 8:00. As I was loading a skid with packed boxes of ceiling tile, I was shocked to hear my mother's voice calling to me from beside an open door near the larger dock opening. Most of the men had hurried toward the break room to grab lunch buckets crammed to the rim with tomato sandwiches, pickles, pudding snacks, and jars of lemonade. A younger man named Cruise, who loved pop music, worked at counting inventory. He was the only other person around. My mother called again. "Doug," she lilted, "Doug?" I wrangled the last few boxes off the line and hauled them onto a skid. The tile-load-out job was messy. A pneumatic glue gun was used to spray each ascending layer of boxes so that the entire skid would remain intact during shipping, and the fine mist of white glue clung to everything—shirts, hair, forearms. It gave workpants a glossy, stiff finish. Work boots looked as if they'd been candied.

I shut off the conveyor belt and walked toward the sound of my mother's voice incessantly calling my name. Cruise was a hundred yards away, sporting a Walkman and puffy headphones, toting a clipboard at his hip as he marked off aisle after aisle of product. I passed through an open area and walked around damaged boxes of tile, and finally to the open dock. My mother stood there in her Arby's shirt, but on the bottom she wore pink, fuzzy, hoofed Porky the Pig pants. She held a heavy sack in her hand, smiling up at me. I climbed down off the dock as she presented the bag.

"Here baby," she said, tired and unsure. "Your mother brought you some of the Beef 'n Cheddars you like." She'd been to the factory many times and knew its layout. I wasn't hungry after loading up on speed, but I didn't want to hurt her feelings and understood I should do a better job of eating.

"Your mother sure would like to see you eat both of those," she said, pointing at the crumpled bag I loosely held.

"You didn't have to come all the way out here, mom," I said. She smiled, the open field behind her head dried and brown, a once forest-colored pasture now punished by the heat. The floodlights attached to the factory's outside wall kicked on, even though it was still light outside. One shone down on top of my mother's thinning hair, lighting up her scalp and giving her the glow of something just starting to ignite.

I sat down on the hood of the car and pulled a foiled sandwich from the pouch. My mother didn't move at all, stayed under the light, her hands at her side, nametag boasting, "Doris! Team #1!"

The first bite of food had no taste; it lolled around in my mouth without giving me the least bit of satisfaction. The sesame seeds became bug-like, almost gagging me as I chewed in vain. When I hit the meat and lukewarm cheese sauce, I realized I might puke. I wrapped the sandwich in the foil and shoved it into the bag. "I think I'll eat these later, Mom." I could see she was disappointed so I came up with, "I'm just so thirsty now. I'll drink the Coke first." She nodded her head, and was back to smiling again.

I sipped on the drink until it gurgled empty, which only cued her to hop to the open car and pull out a two-liter bottle to fill me up again. I popped the lid off and watched as she expertly refilled my drink to the brim; it was as if I was in my very own fast food joint, the only customer.

I drank down three more cups of Coke and looked at my watch. She blurted out, "You got ten more minutes, hon'. Your mother's watching it." She tapped her slim watch to indicate she had it all under control. I began to sense that her visit was planned and purposeful. After all, she worked almost as much as we did, long days leading into nights, staffing the ever-revolving fryers, roasters, and speed cookers at a job she only enjoyed because of the people, and of course, the Looney Tunes promotion that allowed her an outlet for her immense creativity. I decided if I kept my head down and slurped more soda she'd back off, or the time would run out. I wanted to confess what I knew, that dad was most likely having an affair, but I couldn't.

"You seen Carl, honey?" The name made my stomach flitter, as if my internal organs had gotten scared of one another. I'd lived in constant fear of coming upon Carl at the factory, afraid I'd say something stupid trying to help, but only making his hurt more profound. I knew I was to stay away from him, give him the distance he needed, but something in me felt obligated to try and provide some comfort.

"No," I said, my voice crackling. My mother had always had the ability to get me into an emotional state, to peel back the façade and make me choke up. But I had to be back inside the factory shortly, and I wasn't about to appear a crybaby. A large exhaust fan across from where we stood kicked on and blew cool, dusty air in our direction. My mother didn't flinch.

"Your mother wishes you two didn't have to work here." She looked around the parking lot as if trying to find something she'd seen earlier.

"What are those for?" she asked, motioning toward the vans from the asbestos removal company. I realized then that she didn't know. The ruins of an older part of the factory sat sinking into the earth fifty yards away, and for a moment I just stared at the crumbling bricks, the verdant weeds shooting up from an old foundation, bobwhites crying in the undergrowth. For most of the summer I'd been deceiving her, doing drugs in her house, refusing to really talk to her about anything, hiding things. "I think they're here doing some work on the ovens." She stared at the vans while I kept my eyes locked on the ruins in the distance, our gazes not meeting.

"I'd better get back inside, mom," I said. She nodded and walked to the open car door, sat down, and gently pulled the door shut. I started to walk to the steps near the dock when she tooted her horn. I jogged to her rolled-down window and leaned in. She said, "Come by tomorrow if you can. We've got a new sandwich out with white cheddar cheese and chicken breast that you can try for free." Her face beamed, then all at once looked worried. There was a stack of unpaid utility bills near her withered purse. She whispered, "Could your mother borrow a little more money? I need to finish his top."

She pointed to Porky's pants. I gave her what was in my wallet and avoided the kiss she tried to plant on my cheek. I pulled my head out of the car and waved goodbye as she backed up in the sandy lane. Limestone dust powdered everything; the steel structures outside the factory looked as if dingy snow had fallen four inches deep on every ledge, nook, and cranny. I climbed back inside the factory.

Just as my mom pulled away, out of sight, my dad stopped behind me briefly on the forklift. He looked at me with the Arby's bag in my hand, gave me a pithy smile, and nodded. He coasted on by en route to the warehouse. I knew I couldn't eat the food, but I kept it anyway. I looked at my watch and realized I had just enough time to run to the bathroom and throw up, then take a few pills to make it through until morning.

HEAL THYSELF, LOCAL 563 BROTHER

During the second week of class the professor told us we'd need to come up with a project. To illustrate, he showed us yet another film, this one made by his students several years back. "Take a look at this movie to see what I mean by your personal sexual interpretations. In it you will see that several students collaborated on this particular project." He scratched his head through an aged baseball cap, walked across the classroom, and flipped off the lights. In the dark he reminded us, "Like I said, you may choose to do a solo project or pair up, or even form one entire class project."

The VHS tape opened with four male students dressed in ridiculous outfits, white trash bags fashioned to look like sperm. They sported floppy tails and enlarged round heads, slits cut so they could see. Behind them was a row of apartments. The four sperm stood at the curb and waited for something to happen. Before long the camcorder panned up a well-lit sidewalk to a door that had been covered with pink wrapping paper. The door crept slowly open to reveal a large egg dressed in frilly panties the size of a hammock. The egg twirled around slowly to indicate interest in mating as the sperms jockeyed for position, first at the curb, where one fell down and damaged his tail, then again halfway up the sidewalk, where another was nudged into the lawn, unable to right itself and carry on, tail broken off. Clearly the four classmates were drunk, Mötley Crüe blaring in the background. Finally, the last two sperm made it to the door, where the pear-shaped egg was now bent over, a large expanse of white padding ready for the taking. The one sperm punched the other in its big head, and it twisted to the ground. The egg and the remaining trash-bag sperm danced poorly to the music to indicate copulation. Sparklers spit into the frame from off-camera, the silver glints celebrating the moment of conception.

The prof switched the lights back on and began clapping, a sign we were to join in; it was weak, but the class followed his lead. "See," he said, "it doesn't have to be complex. It can even be fun. By the way, the egg in that film was actually a kid from Valpo. He had the costume left over from a play he wrote in which he starred as a gay Humpty Dumpty broken by—" the professor paused and reframed his statement, "—that is, pushed off the wall by society's conventions."

My classmates looked dumbfounded. Since the class had begun, there had been vivid discussions surrounding everything from sex and religion to vibrators. We had debates over the difference in the male and female orgasm and the personal choice, or lack thereof, of prostitution. For the most part, tempers remained in check, but from time to time, after a particularly passionate debate, the professor would say, "See, that's why it's so important for us to have these kinds of dialogues. It helps us with tolerance. Remember that when you fill out the class survey at the end of the course. Universities all over the country want to ban courses like this one." He must have made the same spiel a hundred times in those five weeks. Now he reemphasized our new assignment. "And don't think the project has to be overtly sexual. It doesn't. It could be about certain traits of what it means to be male or female, "Or even," he said, eyebrows lifted, head cocked, "transsexual."

As I walked to the parking lot I tried to imagine what my class project could possibly be, and wondered how I was going to find the time to complete it. The homework had been minimal and mostly essays, which I'd write while on break at the factory or late at night sitting out by the railroad tracks slamming down beers or smoking weed with Jerry. He loved to offer suggestions about the questions, which usually led to some far-fetched tale of him seducing a young woman with his tattoos and heroic rescues in Vietnam. A cold beer in his hand, opening another for me, he'd say, "Read that second question again, I think I got an answer for that sumbitch." Or he'd rub his chin, thinking of an answer even while I scrawled hurriedly in the dusk. If I'd already come up with my answer, he'd insist I read it back to him. One essay question read: *To your comfort level, address a sexual issue in your own life that perplexes you. If you cannot think of one, ask a trusted friend to respond.* I read the question out loud to Jerry while a train approached, its single bright light casting a wide swath of yellow glow as it chugged closer and closer, the thunderous clack, clack, clacking thumping in our bodies like bass music. There was no way Jerry heard it all, so I repeated it again once the train had passed.

I waited for him to respond. He smiled a bit and said, "When I use the shitter, no matter what, I get a boner. Why do you think that is?" He took a long drawl off his can of beer until it was empty, plunked it inside the cooler, and pulled two full ones out, tossing one to me.

He rearranged himself on the overturned bucket he sat on, legs spread. Then he responded to his own question. "I think it's because when I first discovered I could masturbate, I did it in the can, you know, when I was in there to use the restroom. I think the odor acts as a trigger for me." He looked directly at me and nodded. "What do you think, doc?" I told Jerry he was probably right, that our olfactory sense plays an intricate role in memory and association. He nodded his head in agreement and set his can of beer down in a patch of dead grass. He looked around sheepishly and pulled a roach from his pocket, a hairpin on the end. He lit it, took a rapid puff, and got up and brought it to me. Then we took some speed as I folded up my papers. He put his hand on my shoulder and said, "Yep, the old factory sure does cause a lot of memories." I didn't correct him, and as we walked into the warehouse he told me, "Feel free to write that down for that question, doc. The part about the shitter."

. . .

As I got into the car and drove down the main drag that would lead me to the interstate, away from campus and back home, I thought about Jerry's answer, and about how he'd increasingly been telling me that he felt guilty about getting me hooked. When I pulled off the road and into a convenience store lot to grab a cup of coffee and use the restroom, I couldn't help but look up. The gas station had a dropped ceiling with gray MT 454 foil-backs, a rough, all-natural, fissured finish, which couldn't be mistaken for anything but a Celotex product. I stood looking up at the ceiling tile, my head spinning. There they were, the fine products of the Local 563 Paper Workers Union. I was proud.

Even now, every place I go, I look up to see if a bit of us is there. Most of the time, whether it's in a fast food joint in Detroit or a hotel lobby in Minneapolis, the ceiling consists of processed tile with faux finishes, made entirely from a robotic production line. But every so often, when I look up, I see our work, and I hear the voices of men who've passed on, checked out, freely orbiting the unknown, released from the daily burden of a time clock. And when that happens, I remember. And it's the hardest place to leave, harder than I ever thought it could be. Stupid, really, to have only realized this after it was all over.

18

SEE DOUG BE AN ASS

The news of impending war was everywhere. Men who usually wouldn't fork over the twenty-five cents for the newspaper did so now with pride. I was in the break room, waiting to clock out after sixteen hours. During these moments, tired and yet somehow energized that the morning had indeed arrived once more, I imagined a toy rock tumbler inside the time clock, taking the rough minutes and turning them into shiny jewels. As men would file into the break room from all parts of the factory, they'd have the same look of relief on their grimy faces, an expression that indicated an appreciation for the thinnest of reprieves, the chance to live freely outside the walls of the factory for eight hours before returning to do it all over again.

When Qaddafi had a German discothèque bombed four years ear-lier, in 1986, the union men had spray-painted on a large, dusty wall, the words, "No mar Momar!" It was still there, a testament to their ultrapatriotic beliefs as well as a wink at themselves about the way they talked, the dialect that earned them the label of hillbillies. Now, as the Gulf War loomed inevitable, they all carried around newspapers, some crammed into back pockets, others tucked under clamped-down arms or rolled up into perfect cylinders.

One by one the time clock released each man into the possibilities of the day. As they filed out, I waited on my dad. Derrick needed his car for a trip to look at a house he was considering buying. I tried to convince him to take the car back for good, but he was sweet and humble. "I only need to borrow it for a little bit." It was his car, bought on credit through his hard work as an LP tank deliveryman, and here he was asking me for permission to use it. Some memories hurt so much we wish they could be erased, and more than once in my life I've tried to get rid of this one.

The last man clocked out then turned back toward where I sat on a bench. He was a little wiry man with buckteeth and moles all over his head. I didn't know his name, but I knew he worked upstairs somewhere and that he couldn't read, and that his wife had left him because he refused to have the moles removed. They dangled from his cheeks, with darker ones lining his brow and pickling his nose, so profuse that when I first saw him I thought he was being silly, playing a joke involving sticking a box of raisins all over his pale face. Men were always getting bored and constructing something to get a laugh. If there was downtime, if the line or cupolas had stalled, you never knew what you'd find walking into the break room. Men built grills, welded bumpers for their cars, and played strip euchre. They carved figurines from limestone and wrote poetry.

The man looked at me, ill at ease. He held a newspaper in his hands as properly as a child at the teacher's desk, turning in work he feels is not even close to being right. I knew what he was going to ask before his slim, dry lips even parted. Some people can make you see how self-centered you are, and right there in the break room this man's simple presence made me see, even if it was fleeting, how good I had it. His face, so humble and vulnerable, his eyes wide and asking for help, seemed too pure for me. I put my head down and could only see his boots, the tips so worn the steel shone through, a mirror fringed by beaten leather. Finally, we made eye contact, and he asked, "You read this to me, please?" He presented the newspaper, holding it out in both hands. I nodded and he stepped toward me, sat down on the bench.

He pointed with his small finger to the headline story, a picture of tanks rolling through the spot where Jesus once was supposed to have stood. I read in a low voice, slowly, trying my best to keep from looking into his face. When I glanced up at him at the end of a paragraph, I caught his dark eyes darting attentively around my mouth, scanning my head, amazed that a person could accomplish such a mysterious feat. Drugs and booze and a lack of sleep can make you hate the world, especially those moments when someone—a loved one or a stranger or even a nameless, illiterate union brother—shows you what you're missing by staying inside yourself. Suddenly I felt like shredding the newspaper before his face, punishing him for making me feel something I'd wanted to escape so desperately. At the same time I wanted to take extra good care of him, spend ten minutes after every shift teaching him to sound out simple words. "See Dick run. See Jill go. See Doug be an ass."

The man pointed to another story. It was a piece about the local National Guard unit that might be called up. I started reading again, and the man scooted closer to me, his thigh against mine, leaning over my shoulder, trying to follow along. I finished the story and looked up at him again, his face curious, content, and grateful. He took the newspaper from me and folded it in half, creased it like his pants. He stood and bowed slightly.

"Thank you," he said, with boyish timidity. He turned to leave then paused. "You don't sound like your daddy." He smiled. "He reads a little louder than you. Makes jokes too. Tries to see if I'll catch him when he's telling stories. He read me my daddy's piece in the paper when he died. Also read me my daughter's wedding invite." He laughed and blurted out with a much louder voice, "But he wouldn't read me a piece about Purdue beating IU. Said no one needed to know about that!" The smile on his subtle features eased away and he thanked me again, then left through the door, footsteps as light as a barefoot hunter. As if on cue, my father walked in through the back door, went to the coffee machine, and pushed two quarters into the slot.

"Ready," he told me, as he brought the cup to his lips. He looked up, seemingly in a slightly better mood than he'd been in lately, but I noticed that red lines laced into the whites of his eyes, and the lids were puffy. It reminded me of a time when we were still farming and an anhydrous tank malfunctioned, sent ammonia spewing from a broken hose. He jumped down from the tractor to try and fix it, but it was too late. Highly allergic to the chemical, his face swelled up like a beach ball, soft and squishy. For a few days, it seemed his eyes would never open up again, as he stumbled around the house blind, pawing at doors and bumping into floor lamps. He'd always been extra sensitive around the eyes; they'd puff up whenever he was sleepy, or around paint thinner. Exposure to my mother's bleach would blow them up like little balloons. The dusty factory he'd evidently become accustomed to, immune to its itchy residue. Now, though, there was only one explanation for the swelling around his eyes. He was fighting a hangover.

My father stood by the vending machine and sipped his brew, unaware that I knew about his drinking, and in the dark, too, regarding his own son's substance abuse.

My dad walked to the door and pushed it open, held it in place for me to exit. "Come on," he said. "I've got to help Carl with a fence before the next shift." We stepped into the bright sunshine of a hot morning, the light making us squint. A plane droned above us, headed toward Fort Wayne. I noticed another group of asbestos-

removal men in their space suits, working near the back of the factory where I'd seen my dad stash his hooch. The rumor was that they
would have to remove more asbestos than they'd originally thought.
My dad watched the workers intently as they set up a tent not far from
his hush-hush bench. In the glaring sunlight, I couldn't tell if he was
more worried about his secret or the company's.

THE VOYEUR AT THE FENCE

I hadn't planned on sneaking up on them, or hiding behind a large oak tree like a nincompoop. The last thing on my mind as we'd ridden back to the steel house together, my dad's overworked hands gripping the wheel as we took the last few turns, was riding the motorcycle out to Carl's farm and parking it a hundred yards away, coasting so they wouldn't hear me. But I needed to see my dad comfort his friend. If I could watch how he comforted another man, I thought, maybe I could do the same.

After my father had dropped me off at the house he'd said, "Going out to help Carl now. Your mother doesn't get off until afternoon. There's eggs in the refrigerator." He backed the car up and was gone. I walked into the house and sat down on the couch. I tried to nap, even thought of showering to help bring the slumber on, but I always failed miserably at sleeping when the sun was up. Often, when I did manage to grab a few winks, my eyes felt on fire, or the dreams that crept along my screen were terrifying and strange, full of dismembered children and men coughing up black shards of rock. Many times my father's face would show up, neck-deep in some boggy mess, harking up fierce beans that would suddenly explode into tiny versions of his toupee, winged and angry, racing off in a multitude of directions, as he begged me to let him drown.

As I snuck a peak around the fat tree, I couldn't see them anywhere. In the distance, sunlight glittered on the bumper of Carl's truck, the tailgate thrown down, fence posts stacked next to a heap of rolled wire. My father's car sat idle, the front-end battered just like it was when he bought it, mercifully hiding my calf-killing, the start of something that seemed like a million days ago—no rest, no love, nothing in between then and now except extra shifts, drinks and smoke, swallowed pills, and the promise of an end to it all slithering further and further away.

I fished a joint from my pocket. In the thick brush along the road, somehow still green even in the drought, swallows flashed in and out, blasted into the clear sky as a milk cow in the next pasture bawled for her calf. Something at my feet felt awkward, too heavy; I lifted a foot and scraped hot tar from my sole with a stick.

From the house a screen door slammed. Carl and my father walked onto the porch, carrying mugs of coffee. My father looked a foot taller than his friend. They sat down at a gray table, turned their chairs to view the field before them. My dad offered Carl a cigarette and lit it for him. I was close enough to hear their muffled voices if either had chosen to speak, but the summer day was filled only with the chirps of sparrows, the calls of blackbirds at the tops of the high trees. Behind the house the barn sat like a mountain. I scanned the premises for the mower that had killed Carl's little girl. Nothing. Was it in the barn? Given away or sold? I didn't know. I couldn't imagine how my father, with so little use for words, could provide comfort to his lifelong friend, some type of hope or relief that would help keep him from days of despair. What would he find that could replace talk?

By the time I'd smoked the joint down the sun was high in the sky and Carl and my dad had gulped down their last drops of coffee and were ambling slowly down the steps toward the fencerow. Even in the spring or autumn, this type of work would be difficult; one could plan on tender blisters in the center of his palms, and several deep cuts from unmoored barbed wire, but with the heat and hard ground, and no significant rain for weeks to make the digging easier, the job would be tortuous.

I crept around the base of the tree and spotted a stump in a pile of undergrowth. I kicked it free of a tangle of dead morning glory and rolled it with my foot. With the stump against the tree I could sit and watch. The leafy branches of the oak provided excellent shade, the sun breaking through dappling the grass before me with all shapes and sizes of white light.

They started by using wire cutters to clip away the old rusty fence from the rotten posts. My father walked to the far end of the row and Carl began at the other. One by one, they cut the clamps free, working toward each other, and in no time they met in the middle. Next, they worked in tandem snipping the fence into smaller sections and placing them in a stack. They'd worked together for so long, both at the factory and on the farms they both tried to keep alive, that it was like watching a simple yet effective gear-and-cog system click along.

I'd tucked the motorcycle into the ditch and covered it with some hanks of ragweed, but it didn't stop me from worrying that someone might happen by and see the handlebars sticking up and load it into their truck. I rose from the stump and snuck around the other side of the tree, peered down the road. No one had driven past and I assumed the motorcycle was still there, but the pot had turned against me, had me thinking strange thoughts, that a sheriff might find it and come looking for the thief, nail me for trespassing and voyeurism and drug possession. After looking up and down the road again and again, I finally sulked back to the stump.

They'd taken a break. On the tailgate they dangled their feet and drank from a water jug, the sun behind them, the old fencerow nearly gone except for the posts that would need to be yanked out. My dad pulled his Salems from his shirt pocket and pushed two cigarettes into his mouth, struck a match, sucking until he was certain both were lit. He took one cigarette from his mouth and handed it to Carl. They smoked together and drank more thirsty swigs from the water jug. Up the road, a distant motor whirred. I shot a glance back in the direction of Carl and my dad; they'd have to hear it, look in my direction. The rattling noise grew closer, a truck grinding slowly toward us.

As they stood from the tailgate, cocking their hats back to see better, I tried to take cover, placing my hands on the tree and repositioning my body. Then I fell. Got back up. The livestock truck popped into view over a ridge in the road and bore down. I hoped the driver hadn't noticed the hidden motorcycle and that he wasn't fixing to turn into Carl's lane, a maneuver that would surely reveal me. But the truck blew past, pigs grunting and squealing as the driver blew his horn and waved. Carl returned the gesture, taking off his hat and meekly signaling his acknowledgement of the trucker's greeting.

Before long they were back to work, tugging at another section of fence. I watched for another hour or so, the pot working its deceptive ways on my mind. I suddenly realized I was parched; my mouth was dry and I felt dizzy. I stepped from my hiding place and nearly fell over again into the weeds. I realized I'd need to slink my way back along the road to escape. I looked up once more at the two old friends. They were sitting on the tailgate again. I saw my dad patting Carl's back, mumbling something to him that sounded an awful lot like soothing words. I stood stone-still to listen. I wanted to hear those words, take them in and keep them for later. But just as quickly as the image came it was gone again, and they were once more standing together working. Work was what my dad had used, his old standby, to find an opening to help his friend.

As I snuck down the roadside ditch, billowy white clouds moved slowly across the sky, on their way to other places. Carl broke down all at once, standing frozen, bawling. As my dad put down a post and went again to Carl to console him, I wished the clouds would stop, hold their pattern, and give us the storm we so desperately needed.

BUGS IS A THIEF

Back in the steel house, my mother was home working on another Looney Tunes outfit. I sat down at the table and reviewed my notes regarding the class project. We didn't own a video camera, so that option was out. I was a commuter, not around campus to work with a partner, so I was on my own. I re-read the professor's broad take on the project. Sexual behavior in all its forms: biological, sensual, procreational, philosophical, and metaphysical. I heard him in my head, "Use your imagination, make it personal or remove yourself completely, be a part of the project or overtly absent from it. Just make it unique, let whatever form it takes be something we've never seen before."

I doodled on some paper and tapped the pencil on the table. Through the window I saw Derrick's black Monte Carlo pull into the drive. He flung the door open, hauled his big body out of the car, and approached the house in gigantic steps, his enormous thighs flexing, his full beard and bushy yet receding hair flouncing in the breeze. I got up and went to the door before he could knock. With the screen between us, he said, "Oh, there you are. Here." He handed me the keys to his car. Shame worked on my face as I took them, a miniature red IU basketball dangling on the end. He was on his lunch break and busy. "See ya later," he said, his cheer worn down. I watched as he climbed onto the motorcycle, searched the frame for the keys. I'd forgotten and brought them into the house. I skipped to the kitchen table and plucked them from my papers, ran out the door and tossed them to him as he sat straddling the engine.

"Don't ride this, OK?" He looked at me as he pushed the keys into the ignition. "Darren would kill us both if he thought you were driving around on this." I panicked a little, thought someone might have seen me riding out to Carl's. I'd sworn I wouldn't ride the motorcycle after they'd both lectured me about how unsafe it was.

"What about you?" I asked. Derrick revved the motor and clicked the gearshift with his boot; the motorcycle lurched forward and he called over his shoulder. "If I wreck I got plenty of cushion." He yelled louder, "If you did, that tiny ass you got would break for sure." He turned left out of the drive and sped down the street. I listened until the backfires were no longer audible, a slight smile aching at my cheeks. I felt sleepy and wished I could hibernate for a solid month, but I was due back at the factory in a few hours and had to get this project figured out. I staggered to the garage and pulled a bag of pills from behind some pink insulation. I gagged twice trying to swallow them without water.

I was about to open the front door when I caught a glimpse of my mother sheepishly going through my wallet. She took out two twenties and tucked them into her brassiere then hurried back to the couch and sat down. I pretended to make some noise as I came in. My mother had the television on. In her lap she held Bugs Bunny's head for alterations. She sewed the gray and pink cloth, tucking and nipping thread with a pair of small scissors, not looking down at her work for more than a second or two, eyes glued to the TV set. I just assumed the strange little proud grin on her face had to do with repairing Bug's noggin. Often her attempts to remain positive came across as slightly disturbed, overly cheerful about simple things like a new recipe or the forecasted ten percent chance for rain.

She'd resorted to stealing to pay the bills. I sat back down at the table and made sure she couldn't see the course syllabus or the project description if she happened behind me on her way to the sink. My parents had very little idea of what I was studying or the kinds of classes I'd taken; I was the only child to have gone to college, and to them I am certain the idea of a class on the psychology of sexual behavior would've been obscene, so I hid the papers just like my drugs.

I leafed through the class notes and felt the pills taking hold, ratcheting my thinking into frantic loops. Light filtered through my mother's window sheers, amber and thick, as if honey were burbling from the lacy filigree. I was about to pack up all the papers when my mother shouted with glee, "Here it is, baby. Look! Your mother's on the TV!" I was startled and jumped from my chair. I stood at her side by the couch, my head swimming.

She pointed the remote toward the television and turned up the volume. For a moment, seeing her in her Arby's uniform on the TV set was so surreal I thought I'd possibly overdosed. She placed the Bugs Bunny head to her side and crawled up on her knees to listen and watch with more attention.

In the commercial she was reciting a scripted piece. She made grand gestures with her hands to indicate the large dining area and mentioned how the store had won awards for both cleanliness and drive-through wait times. The commercial was over quickly, and she pointed the remote at the TV and shut it off. She climbed off the couch and stood before me. "Well, what do you think? Is your mother a star or what?" She made a pose to indicate stardom; arms spread wide, head tilted, her smile beaming for the phantom reporters and photographers. I was speechless. My mother let loose of her put-on posture and walked past me toward the kitchen. "Your mother's going to fix you a new sandwich we're trying. From scratch. It's got coor-done blue cheese on it. Chicken and bacon." I could hear her fiddling with pans and opening drawers. She would indeed make two of the sandwiches for me to take to the factory for dinner, and after two bites I'd hand them over to another college kid whose appetite was normal. I sat back down at the table and began picking at a spot on my arm, a new nervous twitch I'd developed, my mind outrunning my body by hotly cranked revolutions.

OSHA BREATHER

Upon clocking in, each man was to take a new mask. The union policy and OSHA standard had always been that we wear them to protect our lungs from the rock wool filaments floating in the air and the dust particles on the other side of the plant, where the bevellers and production line cross-cut saws and trimming rigs kept a constant cloud of taupe-colored powder swirling around the fab floor. But the policy wasn't strictly enforced, and often times wearing a mask would get you some serious ribbing, teased about your preference for wearing Kotex instead of a jock strap. But the main reason most workers didn't wear them was because the masks made it difficult to breathe, and during a scorching-hot summer, the only way to cool off was to drink the Gatorade provided by management and breathe unencumbered.

Now, though, even those who'd normally balk took the masks, frightened by the presence of the asbestos removers. These new masks were different from the standard-issue ones, and each worker had to sign or put an X by his name indicating he'd received it. A handout instructed us how to use the device and noted that any questions should be directed to the shift foreman.

The man from the front office handing out the masks seemed uneasy. Mr. Raines had been in management at the factory since the late 1950s and was nearing retirement. The word around the plant was the owners had told him to knock off his chummy interactions with the workers or face a reprimand. From then on he kept to himself, didn't exhibit much more than cordial politeness on the factory floor. He finished handing out the masks and stepped aside so we could all leave the break room and get to our assigned jobs.

My family had known Mr. Raines and his family ever since my father started working at the factory. If we were at the county fair or shopping at Clark's grocery store he'd always take the time to say hello, greet my father with respect. If he had some of his own children with him, he'd introduce us.

At the door leading from the break room to the factory floor, I started to walk around Mr. Raines. He took me by the arm, which surprised me, and held me back as the others filed out. He waited until they'd all slipped by and gently pulled me back. He seemed agitated. He said, "Doug, do you have any questions about the mask?"

"No," I said, "I think I got it." He bowed his head and flattened his necktie, smoothed it against his short-sleeved dress shirt.

"You sure, son?" He held up the paper with the mask directions on it, his hands slightly shaking, a twitch above his eye. Touches of rosacea covered his broad cheeks. I'd never stood so close to Mr. Raines before, and I wasn't certain if I should even be talking to him; my dad's instruction about how to interact with Carl made me less confident about how I was to address any man.

"Yes, sir. I think I got it." I tried a quick smile. He returned it just as fast, and he seemed relieved for a moment.

"Good. Just promise you'll wear it, son." I agreed, and he put forth his hand to shake. I was shocked to feel how cold his fingers were. The factory floor was almost one hundred degrees, and Mr. Raines's hand was so cold it gave me chills. He abruptly ended our handshake and then patted me on the back, holding the door open so I could leave. "Watch out for whatever's tearing open those boxes, son. Watch out." I walked a few steps and heard him say quietly, "Thank you." When I turned to look behind me he was already back inside the break room. Through the glass window I could see him talking to himself.

ZIPPO IN PURGATORY

It was well past 2:00 A.M. when Jerry whistled at me from outside. We'd come up with a signal, a call that was supposed to mimic a whip-poor-will but sounded instead as if a child's recorder had misplayed, off-tune and cracking.

The warehouse was quiet except for the hum from the rafters, where enormous rows of fluorescent lights swayed, dust and dead moths covering their vents. I walked under some railing, jumped over a carton of broken ceiling tiles, and made my way toward the dock opening. My back was weak and the ligaments in my shins burned. Jumping off the dock rammed my knees and for a moment I thought I might pass out. Jerry tried to whip-poor-will again, but it came out even duller this time, flat and lacking even a hint of music. In fact, he really made just a blowing sound, like a little boy trying to whistle. I walked blindly toward him, grappling at the darkness before me, and called his name softly into the clammy night air. Somewhere off in the distance a fire burned, the sweet smell of hickory drifting over the highway and above the waste lagoon.

"Smells good dudn't it? Damn, I remember this one time when I was just a baby really, Daddy took us on a camping trip and we ate all kinds of shit over the fire. Chicken, fish, apple pies. You know them kind you make in those weird little two-sided skillets, they lock down, use white bread and that apple pie filling from the store. Damn, that was good eating." Jerry rambled on some more until finally he stopped and lit his Zippo, the tall flame illuminating his face. "You lookin' for this," he said, pointing to his own head with the other hand.

"It's so dark out here. Where's the beer?" Jerry laughed, a kind of wheezy giggle, and said, "Damn, kid. I remember when you wouldn't touch the stuff." Somewhere a helicopter beat thuds in the dark sky. Jerry said, "You check your mailbox today?"

"No, why?"

"Oh, no reason; you just might be getting a surprise one of these days, that's all." He had my curiosity piqued, but I let it go, knowing that he would only keep taunting me if I asked more questions. We sat down on the large cooler and chugged a cold can of Pabst. In the dark Jerry seemed different, a little smaller, less substantial. As I stood up I told him, "Get your ass off the cooler and I'll grab us a couple new ones."

He took a deep breath and leaned off the cooler, remaining in a crouched position, as if hovering above a dirty toilet seat, just enough for me to get my hand down into the freezing ice water.

"Don't strain yourself, Jerry. I got it."

"Damn, son, I'm beat. I don't know what's gotten into me, but I swear I could go to sleep right now, even after taking some pep." I sat back down next to him and handed him the beer. He seemed to be drinking just as much for sustenance as for the buzz. Jerry flicked open the Zippo again and struck the flint wheel, the intoxicating aroma of lighter fluid like cologne near my nose. The orange glow highlighted his profile and I saw a weakness around his eyes, a sunken quality that I wasn't sure was real or the shadows playing tricks. He held the lighter between us, lowering it until the flame was at our knees.

"Fire's beautiful isn't it? Like I was telling you, that camping trip with my daddy was a doozy. I bet we caught a hundred fish if we snagged one. And the campfires, they were like heaven. You could see your breath if you blew behind you, but your front was as toasty as an oven." Jerry drank the rest of his beer and tossed the can into the night, while still holding the flame dancing in the other hand. He let the lighter go off and patted my knee; in the dark his touch was as slight as a fern brushing against me.

"Man oh man did we have us some fun. Daddy rented us a couple four-wheelers and damn if we didn't ride that hill down to a knob. Brian, that's my brother. Did you ever meet him? Out at the farm?" Jerry answered for me. "No, I guess you didn't; he was already in Pendleton by that time, and you was just a fat baby. Anyway, he was a real daredevil. Loved watching Evel Knievel. We're off running like hell over a pasture and didn't see some barbed wire. Brian ran into it pretty hard, cut his face, right on the cheek, laid it open good. Daddy fixed it up with a kit, but it needed stitches." Jerry sniffled and hacked, spit several times to clear his throat. He said softer, "Even with that it was a good trip. That scar Brian got sure did make him look tough, though. Girls loved it."

He tucked his knees under his chin like he was cold and rocked a little. "I believe that trip was the last time that man ever hugged me, you know that? Wonder what makes us that way, you think?"

"I don't know," I said, thinking of my own dad working at that very moment in the factory somewhere, maybe drinking or drunk himself. Over the months Jerry and I had gotten close, but now, I didn't have any insight to offer whatsoever.

"How you doin' in that sex class?" he asked, a little jab in my ribs to indicate I had it all too good taking such courses under the guise of education.

"Fine. I've got a class project to do though. Don't know what it'll be yet." Jerry stood up and tapped his temple. "My clock says we better get back inside." I got up too and grabbed one last beer to guzzle down before climbing back into the factory. Jerry walked beside me, his arm draped over my shoulder and a cigarette dangling from his lips. He said, "Don't worry about that project. You can always wheel me in there on casters. Call it 'A Fine Male Specimen!'"

"OK," I said, thinking he'd laugh it off. But he was half-serious, and so was I.

"I've never been to a college class before. Could I just come and listen?"

Lots of people monitored classes. Parents, high school students, and even alumni sometimes showed up in all kinds of courses, scribbling notes and taking it all in. It would be nice to have Jerry there, kind of show him off and let the rich students see what life could be like outside the campus.

"Sure," I told him, both of us giggling like little boys agreeing to start a secret club. Jerry put his hand on my neck and said seriously, "I love you." Before I could respond, he coughed some more and the cigarette ash fell from his mouth, a slow-moving ember floating to the ground, dying on its way toward the dirt.

MILLI VANILLI

Cruise was despondent. Three times in a row he'd started to talk, his headphones hanging around his slack neck, but each time he opened his mouth a tremble in his voice prevented him from spitting out whatever it was. We sat on a stack of pallets as I waited for him. He shot a teary-eyed look at me and tried to clear his throat. It was difficult to watch, and I was edgy.

Cruise's love for pop music was matched only by his obsessive-compulsive drive to collect all things related to said music. He wore Vanilla Ice and MC Hammer buttons pinned to his concert T-shirts. His rusty truck sported bumper stickers with the latest album titles of New Kids on the Block and Roxette. Cruise always worked in the inventory part of the warehouse and kind of worshipped my father. More than once he'd winked at me and said, "If it weren't for your old man I wouldn't have this job." He never told me exactly what my dad had done, but I assumed Cruise's current assignment had something to do with it. While doing inventory in the warehouse on the midnight shift could only be interpreted as a demotion, Cruise wasn't the world's best worker, and I imagined a deal may have been brokered that kept Cruise employed, even if it was in one of the crappier jobs.

"Can you turn the music off, Cruise?" I asked, pointing to the Walkman clipped to his wide black belt. I wanted to grab him by his pale, hairy neck and force him to tell me the awful news. He still had his forefinger pressed against his thin lips, as if telling a child to be quiet. He kept his eyes tightly closed, trying to gain the strength to let me in on what was so very wrong.

He switched off a Madonna song and turned to face me, his bad breath almost knocking me over. Cruise pulled a folded-up newspaper from his hip pocket and read aloud, his voice crackling. "'Euro dance band Milli Vanilli admits to lip-synching hits such as 'Girl You Know It's True,' and has their Grammy award revoked.'"

"What?" I said, dumbfounded. He handed me the newspaper, the picture of the duo smudged from his repeated handling.

"I thought I could talk to you about it." Cruise sniffled and shook his head. "I just can't believe it. They were becoming one of my favorite groups. I had tickets to see them with my cousin next month in Cincinnati." He paused to down some Mountain Dew, wiped his mouth and kept right on going. "I mean, if you can't trust singers these days who can you trust?" He became angry. "Shit! I even bought their album for my mom for her birthday. Fuck 'em both! No, I mean it, fuck those guys!" He started to cry and I reached to pat his back, which only made him bawl outright. He sobbed and slobbered and tried to put his head on my shoulder while I made it difficult by dipping my shoulder and inching away from him. But he didn't give up, and tried repeatedly to get me to embrace him.

Down the aisle from us, past rows of boxed and shrink-wrapped skids of ceiling tile, the asbestos removal men were setting up camp. From where I sat with Cruise, the men in their puffy suits appeared as if floating on air. I stared, remembering the promise I'd made Mr.

Raines to wear the mask that now dangled loosely around my neck. Cruise continued to paw at me and pant.

"Where's your mask?" I asked, hoping both to distract and protect him.

"I don't wear those damn things," he sputtered, not interested in discussing anything but pop music's inability to meet his needs for trust and inclusion.

"Cruise, you should wear it." I pulled mine over my mouth and aligned the tight band to keep it from tearing at my hair. In a muffled voice I recited the rules: "Any time you're within their active removal you should put it on. Fifty feet or less."

He stared at me blankly and looked down toward the men sucking the interior of a cargo elevator free of the deadly filaments. Finally, he opened his lunch box at his side and pulled out his mask. Like a passenger going down, down, down in a cursed airplane, I helped my seat buddy get his mask on safely. It wasn't easy. His damn earphone wires trailing down to the Walkman kept getting tangled in the mask's strap. I untwisted them and finally had to unplug the earphones from his belt, an action that Cruise deemed highly threatening. As soon as I'd affixed his mask properly, he grabbed the wire from my hand, shoved the end back into the hole on the Walkman, and flipped on the switch. He struggled to get the earphones over the mask, but once he did, a slinky smile spread toward his curly sideburns. He gave me the thumbs up and strutted into the center of the concrete aisle. He was transformed. His beloved Madonna put him in some type of sloshed state, a drug as potent for him as my beer and weed and speed.

In the distance, the removal men rolled open a section of plastic bubble material to set up yet another tent to cordon off the next area for removal. While it should've occurred to me much sooner, I now wondered just how effective their system of safe removal could be. While the alien ensembles and protective sheathing may have been keeping them from being exposed, the men who'd worked there for twenty, thirty, and forty years were surely already doomed.

Before I started working at the factory, we were always reading obituaries of Celotex workers, the listings of their survivors so formal, using *Mr.* and *Mrs.* to name their grown children all over the Midwest, living in South Bend, Indiana, or Champaign, Illinois, going to college in places like Anderson, Indiana, and Toledo, Ohio. If my thoughts showed through my mask, Cruise didn't seem to notice. He swayed to his music in front of me. He seemed pleased now with his mask, and I wondered if it made him feel like a pop star on a stage; perhaps the thing infused him with a bit of Michael Jackson.

As if reading my thoughts, he did his best imitation of a clumsy moonwalk and slid up next to where I sat. He pulled his mask down and shouted over the music in his ears, now almost psychotically happy. "Thanks for talking with me. I needed someone to talk to, now that demons are tearing open our boxes." Cruise pointed to a freshly dug-into skid, the cardboard shredded. I thought of the Tasmanian Devil. He let the mask flap over his face and turned his music up louder. He jittered and skipped away, down the next aisle of boxes, tallying and recording them on crisp white paper as his ass shimmied to the beat.

24

GOING TO CLASS CLASSY

I just couldn't tell Jerry to change his clothes. When he stepped from his trailer wearing the three-piece suit, I felt a surge of pity. His hair was slicked back, pulled tightly behind his head in a shiny ponytail. The vest of the suit couldn't cover the space to his belt, and the baby blue dress shirt he wore underneath poked out, thin and faded, nearly untucked. He climbed into the car with a beaming smile, but his eyes were tired, gray underneath.

"I didn't think this would fit after all this time, but it's not half bad, huh," he said, patting my thigh. I wanted to protect him and not take him to class with me, but in his lap he placed a notebook with the peace sign on it, as he buckled the seatbelt. He reached into his coat pocket and pulled out some breakfast. "Here," he said, as he handed me something wrapped in paper towel. "You need to eat." I took the warm package and unwrapped it. "I already ate mine," he said. I took a bite of the pound cake with grape jam expertly inserted into a small crack along the top. "Good?" he asked, as he blew his nose.

Inside the classroom Jerry entered and nodded respectfully to other students. If he realized he was the only one wearing semiformal attire, it didn't faze him. He was polite and quiet, sitting next to me while the professor gave a lecture on the differences between male and female refractory periods. Jerry wrote furiously in his notebook and only took his eyes off the prof when he had to turn a page.

After the class, I introduced him to the professor, and Jerry said with pride, "I bet this young man here is your best student." He pulled me into his armpit, the smell of cigarette smoke and mothballs strong at his lapel. The prof was kind enough to agree and asked Jerry a few cursory questions about what he thought of the lecture. Jerry just smiled and said more than once, "Excellent, man. Really, really good." When he shook hands saying goodbye, I couldn't keep my eyes off his askew necktie, as thin as a ribbon, his cough raw and more frequent.

We drove to a restaurant called the Flying Tomato and ate slices of cheese pizza, and guzzled cold pitchers of beer. Jerry loosened his tie and flicked off his shoes. Halfway through the meal he also peeled off his gauzy socks. The place was nearly empty as we sat at a sticky table and talked about the class. Jerry repeated almost the entire lecture from memory, excited and optimistic.

"You think I could go back to school?" His eyes were dancing with hope. I poured us both another mug and wiped up our mess.

"Sure, what would you like to take courses in?"

Jerry acted as if I was playing with him, that I already knew the answer. "Shit, you know, the psychology department." He shook his head, and grinned. "We could open up an office together." He looked off in the distance and pictured it. "We better get going," I told him, and he agreed, flipping through his notebook as we walked to the car in the blinding sun.

Out on the road, Jerry lit up a joint and handed it to me. He turned the radio down, his energy from before zapped. He was tired.

"Shit," he said, watching me take a drag, "I should go to hell for this. Sometimes I picture you as a baby, a little dude tokin'." His face was troubled as he drifted off to sleep. With cornfields dancing along the highway, I drove us back to where we really worked.

SOBERING, TO SEE YOUR MOTHER ON CABLE

L ying on the couch my mind stalled and fretted. I turned over and over, the coarse fabric scraping my skin, the sound amplified in my ears. The steel house was spookily quiet when I finally flopped over onto my side and switched on the television set. I'd only been sleeping for an hour or so, but after awhile, when you've gone without it for so long, your body starts to rebuke normal sleep.

A black-and-white movie about the Civil War flickered across the screen. I punched the remote and sorted through channels. I was thirsty and needed something to calm me, which I thought I could find by watching some late-night television. The channels flipped by, showing bread makers and oldies CDs available with a major credit card, no CODs. *Laverne and Shirley* aired on one station, and the next boasted better-smelling breath by using some sort of tongue scraper. I was about to turn the set off and admit to myself that I could drowse only by smoking a joint, when the screen framed my mother's commercial once again. With the mute on and my mind burnt, I imagined her saying something altogether different than the Arby's spiel.

"Dougie, I know about your druggies. Where you hide them. I know, too, about your father's drinking, and the other things. The killer asbestos. Your mother sees it all. Don't just think she's simply ringing up combo meals at the drive-thru window. She reads the nonstop orders like encrypted messages; the whole town is telling on you and your dad. Your mother knows you hurt, that you've lost your appetite. Come on in for a free small curly fry and let's talk about it. Before you lose your soul, too. I need to borrow some cash. Let me, or I'll take you instead."

I turned the TV off and told myself not to smoke or drink. I would hold out, make a change. I sat up and listened to my own breathing. If I could make it through the early morning hours to dawn without using, I'd be on my way. I surveyed my feet as a distraction. Pale and blistered, they appeared unrecognizable. The pinky toes had calloused-over blisters, leaving dry hard caps on top of raw skin. They throbbed from unreleased liquid. Oftentimes that summer, I'd start to remove my socks only to find the last little piggies had leaked and stuck to the material. Now, I turned on a lamp and pulled a foot to my knee, rested it there, hunching over to get a good look. I squeezed a toe and out came an ooze of infection. I stood and hopped to the bathroom to fetch the bottle of peroxide. I dabbed and dabbed at each little toe, the white fuzz boiling upon application. With the task complete and my toes stinging, I thought working on the class project might help me make it through the night.

At the table I rustled papers and reread the professor's instructions. My father had worked another half-shift, even past the double we'd already pulled; my mother snored alone in their bed. I stood to walk to the sink for a drink, but as soon as the water blasted from the tap, I knew I wouldn't take a drop of it. Irritated, I sat back down at the table and picked at a scab I'd made earlier in the week on my arm, near my wrist. In pictures from this time, my arms look like they're covered in bacon bits. I rose from the table again and went to the sink for a paper towel. As I was dabbing at my wrist, I decided I'd bitten off more than I could chew with this project. A cigarette. I needed a cigarette. I would walk onto the dark porch and have one and that would be it. I couldn't be expected to quit using everything in one night, after all.

The lawn chair on the porch was cool at first but before long my back was sticking to it as I took long drags off the Salem Light. Crickets chirped along the driveway, as chatoyant cat eyes moved toward me, stopped in their tracks, and stared. Out hunting, the cat figured I looked too large to take a run at. I wondered if my single orange cigarette in the dark looked like a long-lost cyclops tomcat she'd once been in love with. I finished the smoke as the eyes moved warily toward the street, the lone lamplight near the curb blinking, the moths flaming around it.

I didn't get the relief I needed. My feet started to take me back inside, but couldn't. The garage was just a few feet away, and I'd stashed a new purchase of weed there just a couple days before. I convinced myself I was being too idealistic. After all, I'd taken speed to work the shifts; it just seemed foolish to believe I'd be able to sleep a few hours if I didn't burn one. Really, what I was going to do was in the best interest of my health. I rationalized that I needed my rest. The class in the morning, along with the drive to and from Muncie, would be taxing enough, not to mention a possible twelve-hour shift after that.

After rolling a joint, I sat out behind the house in the grass, so dry now from the drought it felt like my crossed legs were nesting on thistle. I inhaled deeply. In the east the sun rose orange and pink; a straight horizon slit the sky like a glistening razor separating black from light, now opening a sanguine line to bleed into the new day. The brittle grass around me became an enormous sea sponge. I was afloat on the ocean, the spray never hitting me in the face. Where had the water gone? The vast seas had evaporated, and all the treasures in the new dry world were mine for the taking. I was at home behind the sun. I was stoned.

As the dawn crept over the steel house, the cat from earlier edged by the garage, mewing pathetically, twinkling eyes surveying where I sat pinching the roach. My ambitious sobriety had lasted nearly two full hours. Now I was buzzed and sleepy, which I'd have to counteract with speed and coffee in less than an hour, when I would have to drive to Muncie. I'd witnessed lots of sunrises during the summer, but this was the one to see.

DUDE, WHERE AM I?

I woke up under a satellite dish. I opened my eyes and marveled at the intricate underpinnings, the fretted scaffolding and unusually delicate-looking wires that adhered the disk to the frame. I didn't realize right away it was a satellite dish. Lying on my back, I could see a singular gray color and the webbed steel lace. The bluest sky behind the butt of the parabola gyrated in and out. Shadows fell along my legs but the sun beat down onto my face. I squinted, wanting to make certain the sky wasn't in fact falling toward me.

Slowly I began to piece together scraps of images. I could recall arranging papers at the table in the steel house, tucking them into the manila folder, guzzling tepid coffee from a jug. I saw myself sitting in the class. But how'd I gotten there, under the dish? Nothing about the drive stood out; it was as if I'd been transported to the classroom, racking up attendance points through some metaphysical vehicle. After? What happened after the class? I couldn't focus on the answer. Suddenly, I felt dead from my waist down. Had I fallen from the structure now slowly churning above me? The dish clicked and rotated notch by notch. I shook my right leg, then my left. I could feel my feet, the little toes I'd picked and drained, a good sign.

It's a satellite dish. I'm under a satellite dish. It came to me as I tried to sit up; something smacked me in the head and I fell back to the ground, pea gravel under me. Laughter.

"Hey, stoner! Throw us the football!" More giggling, the kind that's generated when smoking weed; everything is funny and you get it and other people don't and it's because they've not found out how truly fucking fantastic waking and baking can be.

I sat up again. I looked around and spotted the ball next to me in the gravel. It was old and looked like a football they used in the 1940s, fat and bulging. I rolled over and got up on all fours. "Nice ass!" someone yelled; I couldn't make out their faces, but a whole troupe of guys was waiting on me to throw the ball. I pawed at the ball and it moved away; my arms were asleep, tingling. I tried again and finally managed to slide it toward me. I stood up and lumbered away from the dish. I was in a backyard. A kiddie pool with underwear swimming in leafy water sat next to a rusty weight bench. Two empty kegs of beer supported a plywood table, soaked playing cards stuck to the top, where empty bottles of Jim Beam and Jose Cuervo held burnt incense and melted, light-blue candles.

I walked past the junky mess and toward the circle of guys patiently waiting on the ball. As I got closer, stumbling more than walking, I recognized one of them. It was Richard, the guy from class who I'd worked with at the Chinese restaurant. He covered his bearded mouth and laughed as another guy slapped him on the back.

I stood before them as Richard finally got control, just barely, over his snickering. "Damn, you went out like a light, Crandell." He burst out laughing again. "Of course, we all took turns on your rear." The whole group hee-hawed and spewed the beer they drank from red plastic cups. I tossed the football at Richard and turned to leave. I had no idea how I'd gotten there.

I walked toward the house as Richard called after me. "Hey, wait up. Hey." Behind us a boom box blared "Welcome to the Jungle," a song I loathed. The others started to play a disorganized game of tackle football, made almost impossible by their doubling over in laughter every few seconds.

I slid open a patio door and walked inside, hoping the interior of the house would clue me in to where I was, or that I'd see Derrick's car keys with the plastic red IU basketball on them. The den smelled of vomit and smoke. Richard put his hand on my shoulder and turned me around. "Hey," he said, out of breath. "You OK?" His buzz permitted some real concern for me. I didn't answer. Like a thief inside a house for the first time, I looked everywhere, swirling around in each direction, trying to find the goods.

"Dude, if you're looking for your keys, I got them." Richard plucked them from his jeans pocket and jangled them from his hand, holding a cup of beer in the other, his gut rippling over an almost hidden belt. He squinted at me and crinkled his brow, a concerned pothead. "You don't remember what happened, do you?" I'd worn a factory cap, a solid blue one, coarse denim. It was on the table, and I grabbed it, pulled it down and shrugged. It was true, waking up under the satellite dish was a shocker, but not remembering how I'd gotten to this strange house with just one familiar face, the rest strangers, was like sleepwalking or coming to at the gloaming, unsure if the sun's rising or setting, or what day it is, yesterday or tomorrow.

"Dude," Richard said, grinning, letting me in on the joke. "You fainted after class, dude. We're walking to our cars and you just went down like a brick, dude." Richard tossed the keys on the table and pulled a chair out for me; he sat down too, slurping his beer.

"I put you in my car and you woke up and we smoked a joint with those guys." He pointed through the screen door at a set of full ashtrays on the deck table. "See roaches."

I lit a cigarette and the menthol cooled my lips. I was thirsty. I looked toward the sink. "Let me get you a beer, man." Richard walked to the fridge and dug into the crisper, pulled out a can of Milwaukee's Best. Walking back he said, "Then you went outside to piss. Do you remember our head is broken? Anyway, next thing we knew you were asleep under the satellite. I tried to bring you inside but you mumbled something about liking the sky. That was some strong pot." I was embarrassed, my face lit up, as I took a swig from the beer.

"Sorry," I said, sounding as laconic as my father. Richard laughed again and punched me in the arm playfully. "Shit, it's no big deal. Gave me something to do."

I tried to regain my bearings as I watched through the sliding doors the guys running around the backyard giving each other severe hinder-binders. Three guys with no shirts held another guy down and had the waistband of his underwear nearly at the nape of his neck. The guy getting the wedgie didn't seem to mind; he play-acted as if it was just a ho-hum experience, resting his chin on his palm and whistling.

"Where are we?" I said.

"Yorktown. This is my cousin's house. His old man is my mom's brother. They got some money. He doesn't have to work for school." Richard turned to get a better view out the plate glass. "He's the one pulling the hardest on Josh's underwear. The one with the black hair, the one with the earrings."

As if someone had jerked my underwear up my ass, I leapt to my feet. "Shit, what time is it?" I demanded. Richard jumped up too and spilled his beer.

"Damn, don't do that. You scared the shit out of me, dude." He wiped his furry chin and tried to read the time on the VCR. I ran into the kitchen and found the clock on the microwave. It was 2:30, which meant I'd have to drive way over the speed limit to make it to the factory on time.

Richard drove me back to Derrick's car on campus. On the way he told me how he was going to stay on campus and get his master's degree. He said, as if apologizing, "Dude, let's face it, you can't do shit with a bachelor's in psychology or social work." While working at the Chinese restaurant we'd talked on breaks about the kids whose parents paid for everything, as we ate filched sweet and sour chicken, hiding in the freezer so the owner wouldn't cuss at us. We'd only known each other through that job, but for a brief period we'd bonded. I guess he felt he was letting me down now.

"Like I said, my cousin's family's got money, and I'm gonna live there. His old man's picking up my tuition as long as I work in their car lots on the weekends."

Richard pulled up alongside Derrick's car and checked to see if I was OK to drive. I was fine, I told him. He nodded, seemed to know something I didn't. "Here," he said, handing me a paper bag from the backseat. "Take these. They're real good uppers. You better get outta that factory before you die of sleep deprivation." I took the heavy bag and didn't say thank you. Somehow, I felt Richard owed me that much. I believed he'd broken a pact; we'd been in it together, and now he was moving on, passing me by, taking an opportunity our kind rarely got. Before I scrambled out of his car he asked solemnly, "Hey, what are you doing about the class project?"

"I don't know. I can't think of anything. It's just two weeks away, too."

"I'm doing a rap video with those guys at the house. You know, to show how that kind of music is offensive to girls." I should've let Richard know it was a bad idea, that he should use the word *women*, rather than *girls*, and that since all the guys were white it might come across as racist, or that heavy metal was just as offensive. But I had a bag full of illicit drugs in my lap and more road to cover than time to do it in, so I just told him goodbye. I flopped into Derrick's car and started the engine. The parking lot was still, a flash of sparrows dipping out of the sky, landing on the pavement, pecking at some spilled McDonald's French fries. They could go anywhere they wanted, and I was stuck. I revved the motor and did a quick U-turn out of the lot, scattering the birds in all directions, poop landing on the windshield like little bombs. I wished I could go anywhere too. I watched the birds instinctually fly toward another landing. I reached over and grabbed two pills from Richard's bag. For me to get someplace else, I'd need help.

27

PAY IT BACKWARD

That night at work I was assigned the job of toting loose coke rock in a wheelbarrow from a large pile inside the factory to a bare spot on the loading dock. The soot clung to the hair on my arms, but once outside, where a rare breeze wafted off the highway, I felt glad to be working off the line.

By a quarter to midnight, almost quitting time, I'd dumped hundreds of wheelbarrow loads, and my forearms ached and burned. As I emptied another load, I caught a glimpse of them next to a rusty bin pocked with holes and creaking in the wind: my father and the woman—her name was Tina. They were facing one another, their shoulders straight, looking, in the swirl of soot and dust, like two gunslingers sizing each other up before a showdown. Tina was thin and bowlegged, with muscular arms, and she always wore a flannel shirt, summer and winter, and a cap with a heavy-equipment logo on the front.

I slipped behind a utility pole. For a moment, it looked as though he and Tina might simply shake hands, but as the wind grew stronger and a few lonesome drops of rain pelted the sandy lot, my father

151

leaned in and whispered something. He put his hand on her shoulder, and even in the dim light I could see he was talking to her, using words as if it was second nature to him. It felt as if someone had thrown lye in my eyes. My father kept talking, and before I could stop myself, I plucked a shard of coke from the ground and hurled the rough black stone in their direction. As I darted back inside the factory, I heard my dad bellow, "What the hell?" I paused at the door and heard a blood-curdling sound: the two of them giggling, just like my dad and mom had done late on Christmas Eve when they were downstairs trying to figure out how to assemble a toy from Kmart. That laughter had sounded like rain from heaven to me then, but now, as I stood at the factory door, my dad and the woman sounded like hyenas with forked tongues.

. . .

The next morning, my mother was up early as usual, spinning loads of wash, wiping down the kitchen, and preparing for her shift at Arby's. As I lay on the couch, feigning sleep, I spied on her. She wore her regular fast food uniform but clutched four Looney Tunes costumes in plastic sheaves, tags at the tops of the hangers, an indication she'd had the damned things dry-cleaned. She ushered them down gingerly onto the dining room table and shot a glance in my direction. I quickly closed my eye and sucked in a dramatic snore for effect. I eased my eye back to a slit and watched as the little bandit fished the wallet from my jeans and helped herself to a few bills. For a moment, I saw her as a wily raccoon, filching from the very owner that fed it. The phone rang as she bosomed the cash and rushed to get it before another ring came. She whispered, "Yes, I know it's late. I was planning to bring the payment by today." I could hear her breathing, a whistle in her nose. "OK, OK. I will. Please don't shut off the gas. I'll be by today."

Without meaning to, a shrill round of gas slipped from my rear as I continued to fake snore. I saw my mother grin like I was a baby pooting in its diaper. I exhaled an exaggerated sigh and she bought it, thought I was still asleep. At the table she opened her purse, pulled my money from her chest, and slipped it into her wallet. She tiptoed past me to the bathroom and returned with more wadded-up bills. Clearly, she'd resorted to snagging a few singles from my dad's pants too. My mother retrieved the money she'd only moments ago stashed in her wallet and put it all together, counted it to see if she had enough. I suppose they'd lived this way since marriage; my dad turned over his paycheck, except for some spending money, and left her to pay the bills, something that just didn't suit her sense of creativity and penchant for all things arts and crafts. She'd spent the money for the bills on silly costumes.

She opened the door and the bright morning sun cut a swath over my torso. She whispered, "Sorry, honey, go back to sleep. Your mother's sorry." With that she closed the door and the living room was dark again. I decided then to start putting some money into her purse without her knowing it. But it wouldn't fix things. Our summer had secrets, deep ones. Each of us would have to find our own way out, one way or another.

THE FIRST CLIENT

I searched the sheets for my assignment and saw I'd be working as a sorter, a painfully boring task. Two sorters sat across from each other, on either side of a large conveyor belt, as the ceiling tiles rolled off the production line. The job was simple: if a tile appeared damaged, take it off the belt and place it on a skid behind you. Defects could include an unsightly fissure, a faulty paint finish, or poorly beveled edges. You began to pray for screwed-up tiles to relieve the monotony. Otherwise you were being paid to simply sit and gaze at perfect tiles filing past, which felt useless and wrong. Without imperfection, you'd be hypnotized or even lulled to sleep by the line of blurry white tripping past. On the other hand, if too many were defective, you were scrambling like Lucy and Ethel in the chocolate factory.

I put two quarters in the soda machine and punched the square for a Mountain Dew. The new uppers had really brought me to the surface, and I couldn't imagine ever needing to sleep again. I was edgy and soaked with sweat. The last thing I needed was to see Patsy come

prancing through the door, wagging his rear and acting as if he needed to be let outdoors. Larry, his owner, wasn't with him, leaving just
Patsy and me alone in the break room. I was about to ignore him and
bolt out the door when something revealed itself to me. Ever so slowly,
I began to see Patsy as an opportunity, a subject to practice on.

"Hey, boy, how are you?" I said, imitating what I'd heard the
other union men say who had the patience to indulge him.

Patsy whimpered and came closer. After I'd poured beer on him
at the tavern, I assumed he'd hold a grudge, but like all good dogs
he was forgiving and humble—man's best friend. Patsy dropped
his head and I rubbed behind his ears, which truly did initiate an
upheaval of dander, as a cloud of it puffed from his head. The rumor
was Patsy never bathed, and that Larry had once tied him to a fence
post and used the hose on him. Patsy simply shook and shook and
barked and cried until his owner decided it wasn't worth it.

I didn't have much time, so I knew I could only lay the ground-
work. "Come on, boy," I said, patting my thigh, enticing Patsy to
follow me to the benches. I sat down and Patsy ruffed his approval,
stretching out next to me.

"Listen, boy," I said, trying hard to keep up the act, "where'd
you come from? What's your story?" Patsy acted indifferent and
pretended to scratch himself. I knew it was too much to think that I
could get him to use English, even though I'd heard him speak before,
but if I could get him to trust me, maybe I could dig to the bottom of
his fixation. I imagined a childhood wish that was blocked; maybe his
parents didn't let him have a dog, or maybe he'd been an outcast at
school and found comfort in being animal rather than human, avoid-
ing all the social responsibilities that the latter implies.

The time clock clinked away. I'd have to try again later with
the pooch. I stood up and turned to communicate one more signal
of acceptance to Patsy before heading off to sort tiles. He was now
lying on his back cleaning his paws, licking his gnarly dewclaws, axle

grease and wool fibers caked underneath. I reached down and rubbed his belly. Patsy shook his back leg and groaned, perked up his ears. I rubbed harder, feeling his coarse body hair underneath his T-shirt. As I stroked Patsy's undercarriage, I was amazed at how he actually embodied a canine. I'd known he had it down just right, but it took hands-on participation to really get the full effect.

Another story I'd heard around the factory was that one day Larry was playing Frisbee with Patsy in the hummocks near Salamonie Reservoir. Patsy fetched and fetched for nearly an hour as a group of onlookers gathered in a knot by Larry's car. Before long, Patsy was marking his territory, lifting his leg and then sniffing an imaginary wet spot in the short-cropped fescue. Apparently this was enough to send a young mother with two toddlers into a frenzy. She snatched up her babies and clutched them to her chest, running directly to a pay phone where she called the police to report a man acting like a dog and pee-peeing all over the place. The story goes that Larry, who was wearing cutoffs and a tank top, sinewy and tan, drunk as always, spotted the woman on the phone and called his ol' boy to get in the car. Patsy and Larry zoomed out of the parking lot as if a dogcatcher was in hot pursuit.

I told Patsy, "You're a good boy, yes you are." I crouched down nearer him and cooed. I was really getting into it when my dad walked into the break room. I didn't hear him; it was only after a minute or so that I felt him, the kind of stare you can feel climbing up your back. I slowly wound down my rubbing and turned to see my father looking at me as if I were wearing a dress. Patsy, oblivious, begged for me to start again, licking at my hand as I withdrew it like I'd just tinkered with a bomb.

My dad didn't say anything, just plunked his quarter into the machine for a cup of black coffee. It had been weeks since we'd said more than a few cursory words to each other. He still sported the strawlike toupee, and I wondered how uncomfortable it must've been in the blazing-hot drought.

I picked up my pop from the bench and strode out of the break room as quickly and quietly as I knew how. Before the door closed behind me I heard Patsy yapping. I turned around and peered back through the door. Though I couldn't hear him anymore with the door shut, I saw Patsy sit up and notice he was in the room all alone with my father. Patsy stood up and walked to the door like a bona fide human being, perfect posture and all, moving as fast as he could, without a trace of silliness.

NODDING LAND

Celotex managers didn't go to Fisher's tavern; it just wasn't done, and most of the foremen didn't spend much time there either. It was considered the watering hole of the union brothers, the place where we schemed up plans for strike threats, chose the right time for a walk-off, and told jokes about how utterly stupid the men in ties were. Or at least that's what the office lackeys thought went on. So it was odd to see Mr. Raines sitting in a booth by himself, drinking a mug of beer and scribbling on a notepad, his hands red and raw from too much washing. After asbestos was discovered, he started using the restroom multiple times per hour, always scrubbing hard between his fingers with a pile of the coarse, powdered soap that sat in open boxes on the sinks.

Jerry had been out sick for two days, not unusual for him. He often went on binges, running on virtually no sleep, drinking and smoking and popping pills, but, as he would put it, for himself, not for the damn factory's sake. He'd go fishing, or take off to the nudist resort in Roselawn, Indiana, where he'd made significant ties with the owner. Over and over he'd try to get me to go with him. "Come on," he'd say, "nobody's gonna laugh at your teenie weenie." Jerry would crack himself up, and then try to make up by patting me on the back, kind of pulling me toward him. "You could get some ink done there, too." He'd hike up his sleeve and I'd try not to gaze at the faded woman on his shoulder.

Now, without Jerry, the tavern seemed to be missing a key feature, perhaps a back door or an overhead light that had once made the place seem less stark. Men stood in line at the bar, waiting for the owner to cash their checks. He kept plenty of money on hand on Thursdays to ensure the men spent at least some of their hard-earned pay on a few beers. I knew some of the men by their first names, but many of them I'd seen around but never met. The factory is a strange place for cliques. At contract time, or when scabs tried to invade during a strike, it was one for all and all for one, but outside of that, it operated much like a high school. There were religious groups, drinking buddies, the sports-minded, and the outcasts, the ones who read on breaks and those who talked about their favorite sitcoms. The factions were static; men from one group rarely switched over to another. But the common denominator was that each was a member of the Local 563 Paper Workers Union, and that was enough to keep it all together.

I walked to the counter, the smell of sulfur and sweat heavy in the air, cigarette smoke swirling under the lights and the sound of cue balls cracking crisply in the back room. I wedged myself between two men and held up a buck for a Bud. A bartender snatched it from my hand and just as quickly replaced it with an ice-cold bottle. Once away from the throng at the bar, I surveyed the interior. All manner of beer-company signs blinked neon. There was a huge 3-D display of draft horses plowing through a snowy lane, a 1950s-style sign with a hammer and scythe, and a Fourth of July ad featuring a life-size cardboard bikini model that would surely, like so many nights before, have to be wrestled away from one of the drunk men as he danced the fox-trot with her.

My eyes darted from booth to table and back again, each time receiving the cordial nods of men my dad had worked with for decades. Nod. Nod. Nod. It didn't matter how many times I made eye contact with them, the men would give me the same response. It was an unwritten code; a man's son got the full treatment, even if he was just college help. That could be bad, as in the case of chewing on the ass pencil, or good when it came to finding a place to sit down. Any one of the men would've gladly accepted me at his table, but I didn't feel like talking. I wanted to listen.

I walked to where Mr. Raines sat in his booth alone, checking off items from a list. His writing was so tiny it looked like a simple line of dots. I stood at the booth until he looked up, glasses wet from the sweat trailing down his pink head, a small tuft of pearl hair combed over the crown. He smiled slightly and straightened his hunched posture. "Sit down, Doug," he said, as he motioned with his hand, which appeared skinned, like some bony rodent. The deep cracks showed recent bleeding.

I sat down and looked over my shoulder. Mr. Raines was quick to notice my concern. "Don't worry about it, son. Nobody from the office is going to be coming in at this hour. They're all home in bed, or watching Carson." He adjusted a coaster under his slippery glass of beer.

"Why aren't you home in bed, Mr. Raines?" I asked, giving him a smile.

"That's a good question." He didn't say anything else. He seemed preoccupied with the minutia in his notebook. Every second or so he'd glace at it and fidget with his mechanical pencil, letting the lead out, tapping it back inside. Finally, he flipped the cover shut and shoved it into his shirt pocket.

"Sure hope you've been wearing your company-provided HEPA mask, Doug," he said in a robotic voice. Suddenly, he became more passionate, almost seething. "You've got to, Doug. I told them I wouldn't want my child working in a place that's contaminated, but they don't flinch. Even when you ask them if they'd want their family members working in that stuff." The switch went off again, the tide receded. "Besides, you all have been issued your company-provided HEPA masks," he said like a mantra, parroting someone above him. Mr. Raines politely finished his beer and forced a smile onto his face, then gently placed the empty mug onto the coaster and cleared the napkin from the table, wadded it up and kept it in his sore hand. "Well, I better get going, son. Please tell your father I said hello. Here," he said, handing me a dollar bill, "let me buy you a beer." I tried to refuse, so he simply waved over the waitress. "This is for you," he said to her, pulling a five-dollar bill from his wallet, "and this is for another beer for young Mr. Crandell here." She smiled and nodded, darted away through the loud men.

Mr. Raines stood up and seemed lost again in thought. He patted me on the shoulder and headed for the door. I turned to watch him go, the back of his neck as soft and vulnerable as a baby's, all blotched with pink and wrinkled. Through the window I could see him outside on the sidewalk. He paused to fish around in his pants pocket for car keys and then resumed walking, talking to himself as he went.

I was still watching the window when my father walked in. I was surprised to see him there. It was an indication of how much he was drinking. Having a pork fritter sandwich and onion rings with a Pepsi, as we'd done as kids, was one thing, but seeing him in the bar after midnight, sitting down to order a drink, was another. I wondered how much of his bottle was left under the old bench, or if he had to replace it every day or so, like the joints and pills I hid in the garage.

I watched as men shook his hand and offered to buy him drinks. Over the months at the factory I'd been privy to all types of stories about my father, how he helped anyone who asked, and how he might surprise a man he'd not been very fond of with kindness at their time of darkness. I looked around in vain for Carl, knowing he wasn't going to be there, but still I searched, hoping his coming to the bar would be a sign of his recovery, that he'd found a little relief from his pain.

My father performed the head nod and waved off the offers of drinks. He finally made his way to the bar and was served immediately, the owner refusing to take his dollar. My dad sucked down the beer and surveyed the room as I had earlier. I was anxious to see how he'd react seeing me at the booth; I wanted him to plow through the crowd and come and sit down with me, the two of us throwing back cold ones like brutes. Or, I wanted him to see me and order me out for my own good, as if I were still in high school. I longed for him to disapprove and make a scene, drag me out kicking and cursing, while inside I'd be flush with the knowledge that he cared enough to make the effort.

Instead, as he pivoted on his boot heels, reading the crowd like a newspaper, he spotted me and didn't flinch. In the hazy, hot barroom, my father stared directly at me over the heads of our fellow union brothers and did what was called for in such a situation. He nodded at me, and I returned it. The clatter from the bar drowned out the jukebox, as I watched him turn away for another.

SORRY TO HEAR ABOUT JERRY

How many small-town factories still have a credit union inside them? How many small-town factories even still exist? Most are gone, and if they did have a credit union inside, it's now either bulldozed over or empty, like the rest of the plant, mice making the only deposits, little black pellets in a wooden drawer where a child's future once lay.

The credit union at Celotex was above the supply room where boots and gloves and dark blue cupola pants and shirts were issued. A narrow set of steel stairs led to a cramped metal deck, and to the left the door to the credit union swung the wrong way, making you feel as if you'd fall off while opening it and crash thirty feet below. I opened the door and slipped around the edge, trying not to look down. Inside, the room was nearly bare except for a set of hardback chairs and a potted plastic plant on a peeling coffee table, all supplied by the man who ran the credit union, Stanley Brooks. He'd made every attempt to make the place feel like a small branch office of an in-town bank. But many of the men didn't trust any sort of bank, and rumors ran rampant that more than a handful of the workers kept their cash under mattresses or ferreted away in mason jars in their backyards. Some even wore money belts stuffed to the limit, like cobras cinching them at the midsection.

Since it was the first bank I'd ever used, I loved the credit union. Upon opening an account I'd received a maroon booklet made especially for recording all my transactions. Mr. Brooks chose to operate the credit union without the aid of computers, so whenever a transaction was made, I got to watch as he used a calculator to punch in the figures then double-checked it with his own precise math. It was soothing to see him peer from behind his glasses at the figures written neatly on lined paper and begin his tallying. All the receipts were made out in his pristine handwriting that reminded me of calligraphy or ancient printed numerals. His real ink, the smell of mimeograph liquid, and the way he used a small handheld broom to dust the counter of eraser crumbs was worth every stair climbed to get inside the tree house bank.

I presented my booklet. Mr. Brooks smiled and took it from me. He was a quiet man with years of good manners under his belt, and a steadiness about him that made you think of a kindly pastor. I asked Mr. Brooks to withdraw the final tuition payment from my account. I'd had to pay for the classes in installments, and now the remainder was due at the bursar's office in Muncie.

Mr. Brooks handed my money over the counter, and I took the booklet back through a real bank teller's window. I often wondered what he did to occupy his time between union members' visits. I was about to quiz him about his hobbies when he spoke up.

"Sorry to hear about Jerry. I know you two have become close friends." I assumed he was overly concerned about Jerry's normal habit of calling in sick. I tucked my account booklet into my back pocket, half-listening, thinking about how Jerry was probably at that very moment walking nude on a beach, drunk and high, telling stories to the other patrons about how he was helping a college kid with a class on sexual behavior. I said, "I'm sure he's fine." I looked up and caught the somber face of Mr. Brooks.

"Son," he said, "Jerry's been diagnosed with lung cancer. They're not giving him much time at all." My throat tightened.

"I'm sorry, son, I thought you knew. They sent out a message on the union phone tree." I turned and left the close quarters. Out on the metal deck overlooking the plant floor I sucked in hot dusty air. Maybe it was a mistake. Jerry could've been screwing with them, or testing the limits of our contracted sick leave. The huge clock below on the floor indicated I had only a few minutes to get to my job sorting tile. The temperatures had soared in the last few days, and it was well over 95 degrees. Large coolers with icy yellow Gatorade inside them were rolled onto the floor. Off in a corner the asbestos workers started on another section, the plastic tent only halfway up, still crinkly and limp as they attached hoses to their beehive-shaped vacuums. I went down the stairs, yanked the door to the sorting room open, and went directly to my stool. The others were quiet and somber; they'd gotten the news through the phone tree. I didn't make any eye contact as the line began to slowly churn, the noise increasing bit by bit, louder and louder, all the chutes and pulleys, greased wheels and well-lubed saws chirping away, the dust kicking up. I pulled on my mask and waited. The thick silver mesh of the conveyor belt moved vacantly before me; it would be another five minutes before new tiles started appearing. All my mind could hold was the image of Jerry in the glow of his Zippo, his profile perking up as I asked a question in the dark, thinking of an answer that he hoped would help me, his face there and then gone, only a murky shadow left.

THE KILLER IN THE WAREHOUSE

L ater in the night, after the supper break, I was switched to tile-load-out again. I went to work stacking the pallets eight boxes high, four to a level, spraying glue with disregard, coating everything with too much, like gooey snow.

At the supper break I'd smoked a big joint, swallowed some speed, and drunk a quart of cold beer with three other guys as we drove around Lagro, counting our laps, making certain to get back in enough time to clock in and still use every bit of our thirty-minute supper break. In the parking lot, we'd each taken a shot of peppermint schnapps to cover the odor of beer. While cruising around, the other guys, all in their early thirties, the lowest in seniority other than college help, had started in with a reverie about Jerry. They'd talked about his Vietnam heroics, the way he'd always made sure his mother had spending money, and how smart he actually was, mentioning a patent he'd let slip for a hose coupler he'd fashioned at the factory. He'd told me once about it. "Doesn't matter anyway. You sign a paper when you start here that says anything you think up, be it process or product, is the property of the company. Fuck it."

I'd stayed out of the discussion, letting the beer and drugs do their job numbing my soul and brain. The other men had let me be and hadn't prodded me into any kind of sentimental memories.

I walked toward my station to return to work. In the distance I could see the clear tent of the asbestos removers. They weren't inside but someone else was, not suited up in the alien outfit but dressed in a short-sleeved shirt, and no mask. As I get closer I could tell it was Mr. Raines. He stooped and fiddled with the HEPA vacuum panel, flipping the switches and writing things down in his tiny notebook. His hair was wild, and as I approached he looked up, smiled, showing all his teeth, the silver caps and slightly darkened nicotine crevices. He gave me the halt sign and motioned for me to get back, then he unbuttoned the tent and stepped out. "What is it, son?" He was still smiling, as if he couldn't help it.

"You OK?" I asked. "Where's your . . . ?" I said, pointing to his exposed mouth, my question muffled under my own mask. He put his cracked red hand to his face and touched it all over as if he were blind, groping to make out a beautiful woman's features.

"That's funny," he said. "I could've sworn I put that thing on." He snapped his fingers and said, "Poof!" like a magician. We sat down on a skid and Mr. Raines took an item from the pocket of his Sansabelt pants. "Here," he said, handing it to me. "Take this in case you need it." His hot hand placed a pocketknife in mine. It was well worn and smooth. He combed his hair and tossed the comb to the ground. His shirt was wrinkled and I smelled alcohol on his breath, which shocked me. "Here, take these too. There's a mechanical pencil and a matching pen in there." He handed me a plastic pocket protector, packed with an assortment of erasers, paper clips, and toothpicks. "Why?" I said.

He patted me on the back and said with a high-pitched voice, "'Cause I'm going on vacation and won't need them, son." He stood and counted down, "Five, four, three, two, one." The overhead bell rang and the line started up again. Mr. Raines laughed and stepped forward, gave me a quick hug. "When the summer is over and all this is done, come by the house; Mildred would love to have you for dinner." He scooted away whistling, and I noticed he wore slippers on his feet.

As I stacked box upon box I could feel my limbs flail, muscles giving out, and then my arms nearly ceased to move. I struggled to pick up boxes off the line, and when I did finally manage to lift one, I had to use my whole body to get it onto the pallet, employing my groin to hunch the heavy carton of tile forward and align it with the rest, as if I were toting boulders from one pile to another in some biblical story, dehydrated and near collapsing.

I'd accomplished the obliteration of Jerry; now I had to use all my diminished brainpower to concentrate on making my body move. Relief from reality, if only temporary, was enough for me; I couldn't bear thinking of how Jerry had coughed the last time we drank beers.

Finally, the line was clear. I raised the hydraulic lift and pressed another button to push the pallet of towering cartons down the line. As I tossed a new skid onto the rollers, I heard something scratching behind me, over by a skid of ripped-open cartons. I peered through the small window into the packing room; no tiles were exiting the line, which meant I had time to rest. I heard the scratching again. I walked toward the skid and bent down to look behind it. Two red eyes peered back at me. It hissed. This was it. This was the devil everyone had talked about, the one tearing open boxes, waiting to do the same to us, and I was face to face with it. I didn't care. I knelt down and peered back. *It's a miniature version of a man who'd died in the wool mill. He's come back with crispy skin to punish us all, starting with me. He'll cut me open from head to toe with a hot shard of molten coke, the incision smoking as pills and frothy beer spill onto the floor. He'll have me eaten down to bones before the next shift starts.*

Apparently, someone had already spotted the creature and called for help. Before I could get down there and let the thing have its way with me, two foremen with hoes came running down the concrete aisle. They pushed me aside and flipped the skid over, exposing a fat, furry possum, its snout covered in white dust. After all the superstition and scary stories, it turned out the demon was only a nearly blind, matted ball of fur. I was very high and kept my distance from the men who could fire me. I backed up, trying to keep my breath from their noses. One foreman raised his hoe and let it fall with great force onto the possum. He missed, managing only to chop off a hank of hair and skin from the poor animal's head. I yelled a couple unintelligible words, trying in vain to get them to stop, but it was no good. The second man delivered a blow that thudded and then went straight through to the concrete below, making a chink sound, creating a spark. I took off toward my station, where the line was still down. I sat on a stool and thought I might puke. My head swirled. I could hear the men mumbling, and I caught a bit of a sentence. "Least he won't eat any more tile."

I couldn't take being in the factory anymore. It was stifling hot and the place seemed evil. I struggled to stand and teetered toward the large open dock door. I had to gently crawl down, afraid my legs wouldn't hold if I jumped. Outside, the night sky was clear and a full moon lit up the lagoon. The whole area behind the factory had become a home. The patches of dead grass, the rusty pieces of metal lying like dark bones at an archeological dig, and the rails glinting moonlight, all of it was ours, something to hold onto.

I sat down near the tracks and tried to keep it in, but something broke loose suddenly and I sobbed hard, snot filling my nose, making it difficult to breathe. Down the tracks a train blew its horn, chugging forward, closer and closer. The highway was clear, no red brake lights or high beams snaked around the turns. The train gained momentum and thundered forward. The conductor laid on the horn, blaring it repeatedly, little short spurts of an elephant roaring. I looked into the single white eye approaching. As it blew past I wondered if it'd seen me, me and my wet face, dumb and drunk and hurt.

PART III

August 1990

"Remember to be gentle with yourself and others. We are all
children of chance and none can say why some fields will blossom
while others lay brown beneath the August sun."

—KENT NERBURN, theologian

ALL THE HOURS AND NONE OF THE WORDS

eat. Airless and sticky. I rolled onto my side, one eye barely open, and found the light unbearable. My empty, rippling stomach ached. Immediately, I turned the rest of the way onto my stomach and nearly puked. Veins throbbed at my temples as I dry-heaved. Eyes flushed with tears of strain, I rolled over again and wriggled my cramped legs, head pounding. The clock on the dash read nearly 8:00 A.M. I'd have to get on the road now if I wanted to stop at home then make it to class.

Slowly, I put together where I was, still in the factory parking lot, in Derrick's car, hungover. My knuckles were covered with glue boogers; I hadn't worn gloves for the last half of the shift, spraying the pneumatic gun wildly, and the fine hairs on my hands caught the sticky droplets, now matted and painful.

I sat up and looked around the parking lot. The trucks and beat-up sedans of men working the day shift filled the lot. Dirty ocher smoke lifted above the factory into the cobalt sky, the sun sucking it away, blistering the parking lot in the process. I didn't want anyone to see me climbing out of the backseat. I pulled on the door handle and scooted out, remained crouched while opening the driver's side door, climbing back in, and starting up the car.

As I took a turn around the end of the lot and gunned the motor toward the guard shack, I could feel the wad of cash in my front pocket, the money to be used for tuition. I flew through the chain-link gate opening, the tires kicking up dust, loose gravel pinging the underside of the car. Something inside me hung unanswerable.

Out on the back road toward Wabash I floored the car, blurs of trees flipping past, the orange needle on the speedometer rising. I sped through town and took a quick left onto Ross Street. A harsh metallic scrape startled me as the car bottomed out when I swung it into the driveway. I jumped out of the car, heart pounding, and ran up the short walk, tripped over the lip of the carpeted porch. The steel house was sealed up. My hand on the doorknob, I tried it once, twice, twisted it hard, even though it was locked. As I reached for it again, the door cracked open. I pushed it further and stepped inside. My father had his back to me, hairpiece off, only his slick dome showing. He was still in his bedclothes—an IU T-shirt and a pair of khaki shorts. He dipped his head and lit a cigarette. I remembered a picture I'd once seen of him at his high school graduation, standing in a black suit, white shirt and tie, looking out over a wide expanse of farmland in Vigo County. I could never imagine that he'd allowed someone to make him pose; and now I wondered if this was the future he'd envisioned, a rented steel house, extra shift upon extra shift in a contaminated factory, his friends sick and dying, Carl heartbroken.

A puff of smoke billowed from the side of his head. He stood up straighter and sucked in a deep breath, the blast of nicotine providing hope that his own hangover would improve. Finally, he paced into the kitchen for coffee, his smoke as heartwarming to me as the scent of his aftershave; I breathed it in as deeply as he had earlier. Silver bright light radiated over the sink, casting dancing mirrors along the cabinets. I shaded my eyes and watched him stir sugar into a white mug, the clink of the spoon like a wind chime, his hairy forearm flexing. He stood at the counter and gulped down the coffee, filled the mug again, and walked into the small dining area where the telephone sat, recently moved from its regular position on a stand by the door. My mother's lace tablecloth was rumpled, and a single phone number was scrawled on a piece of paper in my father's kinky yet precise print.

"Sit down," he said.

I didn't feel like sitting. I challenged him and said no, waiting for him either to order me again or to tell me whatever it was he'd found out on the phone, a time bomb that had already exploded. He took a sip from the cup and didn't say anything for a few moments, must've looked out the drapes toward the street a dozen times. I watched him bartering with himself, trying to get words to come, promising himself something else in return. I realized we were better at being union brothers than father and son. Something switched along his brow, a tension broke free, if only momentarily, and he thought of another approach.

"I'd like for you to sit down, son." The words from his dry mouth made me want to break down completely, have him hold me until I could fathom more, understand more, but I knew he was lost too, searching too, not able to give me much more than whatever his news was.

I pulled out a chair and sat on the edge of it. A truck backfired on the street then roared past the house.

Quiet. Only the hum of the refrigerator.

"Mr. Raines shot himself last night," he said.

My father pulled an ashtray toward him, orange metallic, marred inside. A matching set of glasses sat in the kitchen cupboard.

"Is he OK?"

"Well, hell no he's not . . ." Angry, he mashed the cigarette into the ashtray, twisted it with enough strength the table squeaked under the pressure. He stood up. The idea that Mr. Raines had killed himself settled into my brain. Dead.

"You talk to him the other night? When you were at the tavern? Couple guys said you did." My dad stood behind me now; I couldn't see him, but the smell of his Salems hung in the air, and his breathing was heavy and faster over my shoulder, the smell of licorice.

"Yes," I said, not able to answer with much else.

"What did he say? He tell you anything?" It felt like an accusation, as if I'd known his plans. I thought of his little notebook, the tiny writing.

"No." I wanted to bury my head on the table. "Do you know about Jerry?" I asked.

"Yes," my father said, a raw faintness in his voice. "He won't be back. He's on medical leave."

I swallowed and began to tell him how we'd gotten close, but no words would come.

For some time my dad simply stood behind me. *I know about your bottle. I'm crashing, too. I can't stand seeing what you've had to work in every day. I hate it. I might stay. I want to run away. I won't finish college. Let's get drunk. Why do we hate each other? Why do I love you? Mom doesn't know about the asbestos. The woman. We're lying to her. She's lying to you. She steals. Was your father proud of you? Only words soothe me. I don't understand why you act so kindly to others and leave us alone. I want this all to stop.* These were the things I wanted to let fly in his direction and see what happened. But when I turned slightly on the chair he was in retreat. He said over his shoulder, "Don't drive like a maniac to Muncie."

I sat and listened to the shower hum. He'd be under the hot steam as I drove to class, working hard to get clean.

PUKING IN PORKY

I had just enough time to stop and see my mother. In the Arby's parking lot, I watched through the plate glass window as she instructed her team of pimply teenagers. She had on the bottom half of Bugs Bunny and was handing a tall kid with a fine mullet the head to Porky. He shook his head adamantly. So did a girl with black roots and thick glasses.

I dragged myself to the front door and tapped on the glass. My mother beamed and dismissed her crew. She fumbled with the lock and twisted the deadbolt both ways before finally letting me inside. It was cool and smelled of French fries. She hugged me tightly and scooted toward the fountain drinks to fill up a large Coke with extra ice, gave it to me with a tired smile. I'd needed to see her, check in, try and make sure she wasn't getting nuttier. I imagined her holding up one of her own staff, a girl that wore Clearsil in pinpoints across her forehead, my mother asking her politely to fill a to-go bag with cash so she could pay the water bill.

"You're gonna be late for your class," she said, wiping her forehead. In the background Mötley Crüe blared, as the kids began stirring the cheddar sauce and firing up the fryers, oil popping like gum. My mom turned and watched the commotion. Without looking at me she said, "They don't like the Looney Tunes. Richie won't wear any of them, and the girls think he's cool so they won't either." With her neck craned, the pale white skin on her throat looked as sad as her outfit. She turned to me and said, "You know, if a college kid wore one, they might think different." Her face lit up with new energy. Without the help of hormones or a good doctor, her emotions could switch from one extreme to another, and now she was as positive and peppy as a new puppy.

"Mom," I started, but she interrupted me with a whine.

"*Pleeeeease!* Just put on Porky and stand by the road and wave at people. Just five minutes." She gave me a pouty look and added, "I can pay you with sandwiches." My mother handed me the pink costume and pointed toward the men's bathroom. "Oh, thank you. Thank you!" she said, clapping and shouting to her crew that I was going to be Porky.

Inside the suit it was hotter than the factory, and my hangover instantly revved back to life. The fabric carried the harsh chemical odor of the cleaners. The eyeholes were misaligned, and I could barely make out the heavy metal headbangers flipping me off as they flew past on the street in pickups and jacked-up Camaros. Profuse sweat crawled down my ass crack as I used grand sweeping motions to entice people to use the drive-thru. A gurgling in my intestines caused me to pinch my butt cheeks together. Something was brewing. A bitter taste gurgled up in my mouth. I swallowed. The top of my head was drenched, my own mullet matted to my skull. I turned to walk up the small incline toward the store. My sphincter pulsed and more rumbling caused me to initiate a tensed-up trot. The pressure built in my rear as I yanked the door to Arby's wide open and sprinted toward the men's room, my mother and her crew watching in dismay.

I didn't have time to yank Porky's head off as I tried in vain to get the damn costume unbuttoned. Frozen, I hoped the lack of movement would be mimicked in my intestines, but it didn't work. I stood in full Porky Pig regalia in the Arby's restroom and shit my pants. My mother knocked on the door and said, "Are you OK, honey?" I heard her crew snickering. I threw off the pink head and puked loudly into the sink, accompanied by the store's trilling Muzak.

SHROOM, SHROOM

I'd never had that much cash at once, and I knew when I hit the campus streets that I wouldn't be going to class. At a stop-light, the exhaust from a semi swamped the interior of the car. I scanned the strip malls for a bar. All through college I'd never had a car, and getting around, remembering what was where, was easier for me on foot; my frame of reference was all off inside the car. The amphetamines I'd taken on the way to Muncie caused my knees to knock, and I couldn't sit still behind the wheel. I thought of turning around and still trying to make it to class, but the thought of planting myself at a desk was enough to propel me further along the street.

At a fork in the road, something seemed familiar. I made several turns, now recalling some of the landmarks: the banks of the White River, a three-way stop, a gas station with an enormous Sweet Six-teen banner still hanging in the window. I gathered my bearings and bore down a street to a final turn, past a chain-link fence and a bar-becue restaurant.

The parking lot held a few 4x4s, a couple vans, and a herd of motorcycles. The place was called the Hunters Lounge, a dive bar where I'd had an occasional beer during college. I'd stop in with a few friends after we'd finished shifts at whatever fast food joint we were temporarily working in to make rent payments.

I walked to the door and yanked it open, took a hesitant step inside. The darkness stunned me. My eyes couldn't adjust, and I had to stand perfectly still until the bar came into focus, the blinking jukebox and a bulb in the hallway leading to the one bathroom. I made my way to the bar and ordered a pitcher of beer, but was told serving pitchers was against the rules unless I had two or more in my party. The waitress, who had crinkled skin and beautiful white teeth except for one dark one at the corner, told me, "But I can pour six mugs into a pitcher and sell it to you that way. Costs two dollars more, hon'."

"Fine." I lit a cigarette and watched her judiciously fill a mug six times then empty it into a plastic pitcher. When she returned she asked if I needed a menu. "No," I said, "thank you." She faked a quick smile and went back to cleaning behind the bar, a talk show on the TV, her eyes only looking away from it when she couldn't find by touch the bottle of blue cleaner on the shelf near her ample hip.

I drank down a mug and filled it again, scanned the bar to see who else was drinking this early, what other patrons might be putting something off, trying to find a place to hide out, or fine-tuning a coping system. In a far corner the men who evidently owned the motorcycles sat in a large semicircle, popping shooters and sharing several pitchers. Along the other side of the bar two old men with weathered hands drank together, snapping peanut shells and tossing the bare treats into their whiskery mouths, not saying a word, passing the newspaper back and forth. At two different tables, sitting separately, a man and a woman slouched over their drinks, smoking, eyes red, waking up or staying up or trying to get to sleep.

I looked at my watch. The class would be halfway over by now, and I'd be marked for an absence. The progress of our projects would be the main topic of discussion; the professor would ask if anyone needed help, an idea. I should be there, I thought; I need help.

Behind me a few stragglers played pool. They were uneasy with one another; while one took his shot at the table, the other two stood with hands shoved in pockets, a pick-up game of strangers, a chance to pass the time, to not feel too alone in drinking before noon.

I reached down and touched the large wad of money in my pocket, a thick packet of opportunity, eight hundred dollars. I could steal my own brother's car and flee, end up somewhere in Georgia before the money ran out, leave the class and the factory and the measly bachelor's degree behind, escape the death at the factory. Of course, that would take guts, require me to take action, move from the barstool.

The pitcher was nearly gone when I got up to pee. The one urinal hung loosely off the wall, and when one of the motorcyclists burst in he had to wait for me to finish. He took a step back and leaned against the wall, smoking and chewing gum at the same time. I didn't want to talk. I kept my head tucked down, watching myself. He spoke up, "Damn, they should get a few more pissers in here, heh?" I nodded slowly. The man flipped his cigarette into the sink, spit his gum out, and proceeded to hark up a large loogie. It sounded like a piece of raw meat hitting the floor.

We traded places, and I thought I was safe from having to talk anymore when he said, "Come over to our table. A kid shouldn't be drinking by himself."

At the round table I sat uncomfortably, the others smiling and nodding. As a group they had the smell of leather and recently passed gas, their stomachs upset from too much road food and even more beer. Naïve, I believed they were Hell's Angels. I thought of Derrick riding his little hog, its small frame bending under his girth, the handlebars low enough for a trike. The man from the bathroom ordered another round of pitchers. He said, "This is my friend from the pisser." He laughed and tossed back a whole mug in one drink. "Must be a college kid," another one said, his white mustache greased into sharp points. I nodded, took a drink, waited for something to come, felt it looming.

Before long the bikers' shirts were all turning the same color, then they were floating into the paneled wall behind them, wood grain covering their faces. My brain did somersaults. The man from the bathroom said, "He's shrooming. Just sold him some in the crapper." He got up and walked over next to me, pulled out a chair that swam in the air, the legs forming fins. I was hurt that my new friend would drown a fish in oxygen, as he sat on the poor thing. He put his hand on my shoulder. "Listen, it's just a trip. Don't forget that. You're tripping, and that's OK." His words spun, repeated, stuttered like a record skipping. He was the captain. I pulled the mug to my face to take a sip, but the man swiped it away, put it on the table behind him. "No more beer. Might get sick." The music in the background walked right into my head, played just for me, the bass singing directly to the snail, the cochlea, in my inner ear. My hidden snail, and the legged fish my friend had squashed with his ass, made me sad.

Bad trip. Kid's freaking out. Snail. Fish. Bass. Ass-BASS-toes. Fish fly in water. Doors jammed. It's Mr. RAINE-ING. It's pouring. Your old man is dying. Get him up. Up. Up. Motel. To the motel. Lot. Lots. Across the lot, hot lot, lots of hot. Good thing the motel's right here. Clock in. Clock out. Check out's at noon. Check out for good. Put on MTV, they like that. Put him in the bed. Let's get out of here. Comforter like a sheet of ice, pretty horses above the bed, rearing up, stampeding over my ice-covered groin.

Hours passed in the motel. I heeded the older man's advice, kept telling myself it was just a trip, and as each minute swam away, corded off from its swarm, its school, I dog-paddled toward the shore, even though at times I drowned over and over.

I've often wondered how I had the ability to manage the streets toward the bursar's office. Walking and walking and taking turns, most likely the longest route possible, moving from city to campus, swerving from the hot sidewalks into shortcuts over soft, grassy knolls, through familiar back lots and homey alleys, places that resounded with more music just for me, those voices from the easier years, friends that had dropped out, not made it, home in Indiana towns working in Olive Gardens and First National Banks.

At the doors leading to the financial office, I walked right into the glass and bloodied my nose, ready to make the final payment on my education.

PAPER AND FIRE

It was nighttime at the factory. A few men had planned a candlelight vigil for Mr. Raines on the docks out back. I held a short, used votive. The others had brought longer sticks, and they looked more respectful. My candle was too low, didn't flicker nicely in the hot breeze. Someone spoke respectfully and a prayer followed, as doves cooed in the low-hanging vines tangled at the end of the lagoon. A bright sliver of moon cut a portal in the sky. Swallows swooped down from the air as if falling from a plateau, nabbing insects and racing upward once more. We were on a break, only fifteen minutes, and while the informal ceremony was dedicated to Mr. Raines, Larry said a few words for Jerry as well, Patsy obediently at his side on all fours. "Let's also ask that Jerry be healed and lifted up. That he find comfort and peace. Amen." One by one each man blew out his candle as the bell rang inside, indicating the line was about to start again. Everyone filed through the open door, tucking candles into hip pockets, each replacing his mask.

With the news of Jerry and six others out sick, all the union brothers had started wearing the masks, sometimes even on breaks and at lunch. A few even ate with them on, lifting the masks only long enough to stuff food into their mouths. They were all about taking precautions, even though their coworkers had been dying for years already. As if all the time spent sucking in the factory air hadn't already done its damage, as if the only thing to be concerned about was the breathing, the daily benedictions and prayers each said before leaving home. *Let me see her graduate. Just wait until I can get my pension. Give me a few years with the grandkids. Not until there's a little saved. Let me take the wife out west before it's over.* Words mumbled as they drove the potholed roads to their place of work, the faithful structure housing their modest hopes, poisoning them at the same time.

Back on the job I worked under the influence. It'd been two days since the mushrooms episode in Muncie, and my body had recovered enough to abuse it again, drinking shots off the dock in the dark. If it had still been light outside, I thought, I could have squeezed behind some rusted relic hanging from the old factory wall, as I slugged back the booze, peeking through a slat, spying on my dad as he drank too, the woman next to him, the two of them giggling. If I could only catch him alone, near the tracks, one shove would do it. He deserved to be contaminated.

With the line down, I scrawled words on a slip of paper, nothing of substance, just random thoughts, hoping something would come to me for the class project, trying hard not to think of Mr. Raines or Jerry, or anyone else for that matter. I stood up and tucked the piece of paper in my back pocket, walked toward the wall and fiddled with a sheath of cardboard stuck behind a piece of sheet metal, pulled it out. In all sorts of handwriting, printed and cursive, in ink and in pencil, there were phrases written on the cardboard. One read: *Silence is golden*, another, *Make love, not war.* Up and down the edges were more quotes. *He who seeks shall find. This job sucks! No rest for the weary* and on and on. Some were signed while others were anonymous. Most were clichés and some original. A few naughty limericks filled the top corner, and some Bible verses had been pressed hard into the cardboard, pencil lead infused deep. A few passages had times written by them, and most had been dated. I'd worked the tile-load-out job a lot and had never noticed the thing stuck there.

I sat down and held the cardboard before me like a large easel, tipping it just right to reduce the glare from overhead. One entry near the top was dated April 1972. It read, "Things come and they go, but this place goes on forever." An arrow drawn with a magic marker pointed down through all the other words and verses and slanted sentences to an opening where the author inscribed his name. At the arrow tip, the name Jerry was printed, his employee number next to it like a POW. Something about Jerry's words from nearly two decades earlier resonated in me, sparked an idea.

I rummaged through the station desk and found a legal pad, the sheets rumpled from water damage; a few brown coffee stains like Olympic rings covered the first page. For the next hour or so I copied down all the writing, along with dates and times. When the fab line started back up, I'd gotten them all down, transcribing as fast as I could. Fully counted, back and front, the cardboard held nearly two hundred inscriptions. It took up five pages of notebook paper. I started to tuck the board back in its hiding place, but something made me stop. I sat down on the stool and thought for a moment. I didn't want some deep collegiate thought to take up the limited space on the board. I didn't want a lyric or stupid saying either. Finally, I came up with *Live and Let Live*. I printed it solidly in blue ink, dated it, wrote my name, and drew a peace sign. True, it wasn't highly original, but it was something to leave behind for others who'd stumble upon the secreted-away tablet.

Only members of the United Paper Workers Union would choose pressed pulp fiber cardboard to hold their ancient scripts, their advice, musings, and farewells. Who knows, maybe fire doesn't really destroy paper, maybe it just transforms what's written on it into readable smoke, plumes traveling up to the heavens, reconstituted into something more durable, a multitude of prayers, where they live on forever.

36

GIFT SUBSCRIPTION

An orchard. The trees were past fruiting; only a few shriveled pears dangled like long-dead mice, the stems the crisp tails, always the last to fully decompose. The summer drought had been hard on everything—trees, grass—and the corn and soybeans that shouldn't turn tan until after the first frost looked as though they'd already been through winter.

I shuddered when I lit up a joint; drop it, and the whole orchard would go up in flames, maybe even the entire countryside. I recalled my father's technique and, for the first time in my life, rolled my right jean cuff into a deep pocket, let the ashes fall into it. My back against the base of the tree, wood knots grinding my vertebrae, I sucked in and held my breath, looking around to make sure I wasn't being noticed. Above me an oriole flicked dun straw from a delicate nest. A few downy feathers floated away; I watched them until they were no longer visible. The book bag at my side held the reason for my pilgrimage.

Contents of said book bag:

a fifth of vodka
several prerolled joints
speed
class project notes
application to graduate from Ball State University
a magazine

The bird above my head continued to peck and toss. To delay opening the backpack, I studied her movements, the way her head clicked mechanically from side to side, small black eyes like polished pebbles. The bird's legs were gray and spindly, seemingly hardly enough to land on, or to keep her upright as she hopped from the old nest to a bough no bigger than a wire. How do birds remain alive while men die? Surely, they're at greater risk, up against BB guns, pesticides, glass windows, cats, and disease. Yet I'd walked through acres and acres of farm fields and had seen maybe five dead birds in my whole life, whereas twice that many Celotex men had died every year for as long as I could remember. Birds don't make ceiling tile; maybe that was it. The pot had fooled me again into believing I was onto something profound. I took another hit, and another, the roach burning my fingertips.

Was it safe to open the bag? I unzipped it and quickly plunged my hand in, felt around wildly for the vodka. One big swig, and it burned, another, and the fire from the first drink fought the new flame. I thought of how men out west deliberately set fires in order to stop them, one orange ring flaming outward to confront a bigger one coming in.

With the bottle between my legs, I was as ready as I would ever be. I reached into the backpack again and pulled out the magazine, or rather a journal. It was the surprise Jerry had taunted me about. Jerry's gift to me. During my years in college I'd thumbed through back issues of this journal, but I'd never owned one, or even known anyone who had a subscription. I assumed maybe my professors did, or were expected to, or requisitioned one in their names through the departmental budget. But there it was, right in my hands, the heavy stock cover with the title, *Psychological Bulletin*, printed on it, the black ink thick.

I turned the journal over in my hands and flipped through the back pages. Terms I'd never understood in class, like *chi-square, two-nested models, correct specification*, and *misspecification* flipped past. What would Jerry have had to go through to find out how to buy me a subscription? I pictured him slinking into the library, asking a woman with horn-rimmed glasses for help. "Got this kid I've known since he was a baby. He's getting a psychology degree. What kinda publication you got in way of that sorta thing?" I saw him tonguing the stray mustache hairs at the corner of his lip, a nervous tic, something he did when he wasn't sure of how he was being perceived. When he was only a tough-looking grown-up to me, I'd never dreamt he could be unsure about anything, but as I'd gotten to know him, I'd discovered a man with deep-rooted insecurities, illogical phobias, intimacy failures, and other character flaws. Just like me.

The orchard was a perfect square, fenced in and platted on all sides. I remembered passing it as a kid, on the way to the factory to deliver food to my father, how the little fruit trees in the center, surrounded by more mature ones, could hardly be seen. A man and woman, white-haired but strong and upright, would be climbing ladders, hauling round wooden baskets at their hips, often smiling at one another, and I'd imagine they were playing a game to see who could fill theirs the fastest. Sometimes, I'd see the little trees supported by wire and tubing, protected from the elements. The large trees, I believed, were the parents of the babies in the middle. I also thought gravel had big-brother stones, and that the boulders in the fields were parents and grandparents.

I took another drink and put the bottle and the journal back in the bag. I'd hoped the time in the orchard would give me the courage I needed to drive another five miles to Jerry's rented trailer and see him for the first time since he was diagnosed, but I was left with only a mild buzz and a crick in my back from leaning against the tree. I stood up and swung the backpack over my shoulder. It dawned on me that I was being too brazen; after all, I was certainly trespassing, and the contents of my bag would get me in deep shit if the county sheriff was called, maybe the same ones that had gotten so choked up years earlier when my cooler contained only brownies and milk. I'd be such a disappointment to them, their brownie boy all high and strung out, encroaching on a desiccated orchard, his breath laced with liquor, not the 2 percent, homogenized, pasteurized, grade-A milk that had hotly exhaled on them as he confessed to having had no fun whatsoever at the reservoir party.

In the car I started the engine and eased the front wheels onto the pavement, leaving the dry grass. Determined, I sped up and headed toward Jerry's place. I thought of the class project and the cardboard tablet I'd found. It was odd to be feeling a tinge of optimism, a slight enthusiasm about an idea. I rounded a turn in the road and saw Jerry's trailer sitting like a Lego in the distance, small and rectangular, a bar of white in the wide open terrain, only rusted farm implements and dots of cattle surrounding him in all directions, clomps of dead grass and cow pies drying in the hot sun, hundreds of them like land mines over the paltry ground.

I pulled over onto the shoulder and turned the car off. The road straightened out before me, the nose of Derrick's car pointing right at Jerry's mobile shack, its wheels visible, no skirting to give the appearance of permanence. I started the car again and put my foot on the brake, yanked the gearshift on the steering column, the needle set on D. From the other end of the road I saw a vehicle approaching. It was far enough away to look like a bug. I shoved the car back into park and waited. If I stayed there they'd probably pull over, but if I took off now that would likely raise suspicion too. I reseated the cap on my head and grabbed for the registration under the sun visor, tucked it into my waist, and slung the backpack over a shoulder. The oncoming car wasn't moving quickly but it had its headlights on, a sign it could be the county sheriff. I opened the door and rolled out of the car and into the shallow ditch, crawling on all fours until I reached a deeper section. I was GI Joe in union clothes. Pausing, I raised my head to peek over the lip of parched earth. The car coming from the other direction was still a good bit away, not close enough to see who it was.

I decided to head toward a shank of trees jutting out from the corner of the field. True, if it was a cop, it would be the first place he'd look, but he also might just drive on by, thinking someone was out hunting squirrel or taking a lover's stroll. I crawled to the edge of the slim poplars and slipped inside their cover. Finally, the car pulled into Jerry's dusty lane. As soon as the vehicle had made its right turn, I knew it was my dad. Even under the cooler canopy of shade I felt my face redden; this made two times in the last month that I'd spied on my father as he visited union brothers. I was beginning to think I was a stalker. I trudged back to the car, no fear now of being busted by cops.

My dad stood on the wobbly two-by-four deck of the trailer and knocked on the door. I'd been in a hundred trailers like Jerry's, at sleepovers as a kid. So I knew when my father pounded on the door again that the walls inside Jerry's place were rattling to beat all hell, as if a tremor had commenced, the ground shifting underneath.

I put the car in neutral and used my foot to paw it forward, inching it closer and closer without making much noise. I wanted to see as clearly as I could if Jerry opened the door. I wanted to talk with him, but I was scared too, afraid that I couldn't help him. Before long I was close enough to see the license plate clearly on my dad's car.

A large oak tree, growing nearly into the road, helped camouflage me. I peered past its large trunk at my father still standing on the creaking deck. He clutched something against his chest, a Crock-Pot I recognized as my mother's, white with wide bands of olive green and rusty orange, a relic of the 1970s. She'd made a thousand meals in that thing for my dad, toting it out to the factory with a basket of corn bread or yeast rolls or flaky biscuits.

My dad looked in the other direction when he knocked one last time, squinting at the cattle in the distance. Finally, the door opened just a crack. Jerry's face, the same as always, popped out. Dad took off his hat and, with the crock tucked in at his waist, stepped inside, and the door closed. And that was that. The man I'd spent hours upon hours with over the months, the person I had tried to summon up the courage to visit, had welcomed my old man into his home, into his illness. It was the very thing I'd wanted to do, but I was too late, too cowardly. And I knew better than to try and weasel my way inside now, certain my dad would consider Jerry's situation just as off-limits as Carl's. I started up the car and performed a sloppy three-point turn, the hot tar on the pavement making little snapping sounds as I slowly rolled away, carrying with me Jerry's gift.

37

NIGHT LIGHTS

Management was angry. New policies appeared, spelled out in typewritten memos, regarding safety, break time restrictions, and the use of company products (more than a few men pilfered MT 454 foil-backs, the standard ceiling tile, for their basements, their brother-in-law's workshop, or their parents' new addition). The crisp memos were posted in the smelly bathrooms, others pinned to the job board in the break area. Mr. Raines's death had been a blow, a sign that even their own men could die, and the front office mourned by striking back, or at least that's the way it appeared to me. The removal of the asbestos was nearly complete, and every union brother was required by management to wear a mask at all times.

It wasn't put in writing, but rumors spread across the plant floor that management was also serious about drinking on the job. The word was that anyone found with even a little bit of alcohol on his breath would meet with serious consequences. In short, the company had to show that it was dealing with problems, any problems, with an eye toward the safety and protection of its workers.

That night, out by the railroad tracks, I cracked open a beer and sipped the froth from the lip. I'd gotten to stay on the tile-load-out job, the kind of isolated work I enjoyed most. The August nights had begun to act as broilers; the smokestacks spewed out clouds of dust that held the heat from the day close to the old factory, baking everything. I leaned against the wall and surveyed the college graduation application on a clipboard in my hand. You applied to get in, and again to get out. Strange. I wrote neatly on the form and checked off boxes, agreeing to receive my real diploma in the mail four to six weeks later in the event that I failed to pass any remaining classes. This was not how I'd imagined my college life ending, sitting behind an ailing factory, slurping beer, and listening to yet another train approaching. Two docks down, in the full light of an overhead high beam, I could see Patsy on all fours, Larry having him perform tricks for the barbecue potato chips he doled out at each successful attempt to sit, roll over, and beg. A group of college kids and the men who found it funny all gathered around in a circle, clapping and yelling requests. "Make him take a shit!" "Have that son-of-a-bitch go fetch his own dick!"

I scrawled my Social Security number in the boxes provided and signed the last page. Below it a statement read: "If you plan on going through ceremonies, arrive at noon on the day of graduation to receive your cap and gown." It hadn't occurred to me to walk on stage and get my diploma, a fake one at that, but still, something about the image made me sit up straighter. I was deep in thought when I heard someone say from behind me, "You best not let anyone see you out here with beer, son." I turned to see a shadowy figure climbing slowly down from the dock's edge. I pushed the remainder of the six-pack into a large divot behind me. I stood up with the papers in my hand as the dark outline dragged its feet toward me. A ray of light from the approaching train finally lit him up. It was Henry. He smiled broadly, carrying a paper sack in his black hand.

The train swept past us, cars clacking rhythmically, the smell of hot oil and creosote rushing by too.

"Thought you could use some grub, son," he said, his black hair freshly combed, and a pair of safety glasses as big as saucers over his dark eyes. I'd not worked with Henry for weeks, and now, he was offering me food.

"I fixed an extrie sandwich for ya. Hope you like ham loaf. It's got pimento in it." He handed me a soft white-bread sandwich wrapped in clear plastic and tied with a twist. Henry said, a bite already in his toothless mouth, "Been noticing you've dropped some weight, son." He chewed slowly and motioned for me to sit back down. I held his gifted sandwich in my hand and couldn't think of any way to get out of eating it. I wasn't going to hurt Henry's feelings, so I started to unwrap the soft, slightly chilled packet in the dark. The electric lines just past the tracks buzzed, and a transformer near the top suddenly popped with silvery sparks; they drifted toward the ground, the stink of burnt wire wafting toward us.

"I'll be damned," said Henry, a wad of food in his mouth like chaw. "Must been a wreck up the line somewhere, probably hit a pole." One of the hefty motors running the line stalled, then failed, a nice silence overtaking the night. One by one, different parts of the factory went dark. In just a few minutes the whole place was like a haunted house. It wasn't the first time the plant had slipped into a temporary blackout. The men loved it. When the lights went out at Celotex they all turned into kids. The linemen would creep around in the dark and poke their heads into different rooms, shining a flashlight under their chin, giving college kids and newbies the fright of their lives. Larry liked to have Patsy act as if he were a cadaver-sniffing dog, searching out victims lounging in the break room or sitting on the toilet. Of course, some men, like my father, found it all silly and a waste of time, but for most workers blackouts were a welcomed respite from the daily grind.

Henry leaned on me briefly and said, "Not so bad, huh? Get paid to sit in the dark. They won't have the whole place up and running for a while, even if the lights come back on right now." He always smelled the same, a mild staleness combined with the red and white peppermint candies he ate all the time. Even while he gummed the pimento sandwich I could still smell the candies. Finished, he balled up the plastic bag and shoved it into the paper one.

Henry pointed to the sandwich sitting idly in my palm. "You gonna eat that, son, or marry it?" He dug a hand into his shirt pocket and pulled out his false teeth; they made a clacking sound as he pushed them into his mouth, lips smacking, a peppermint unwrapped and inside so quickly his suckling gave the impression of a baby that hadn't nursed in a day.

I put the sandwich to my lips and nibbled. Henry said, "Boy, I can't tell you how glad I'll be to get out of this place. It won't be long now. I retire in six months." He sighed deeply, a rattle in his chest. Henry smoked two packs of cigarettes a day, most of the time with one of those candies wedged inside his jaw, wallowing it around as he puffed, clicking against the dentures. Behind us a few high-pitched screams rang out. I could just see the memos that would be posted tomorrow about the zero-tolerance stance the company was taking on tomfoolery: *There will be absolutely no goosing, hinder-binders, wet-willies, and/or playful ribbing near the buttocks. None.*

I forced myself to take another bite of the sandwich. Something rustled in the dead weeds next to an old oil drum. The sounds that had been there all along could be heard more easily now, the old factory made still. Rusted hinges whined; a shoddy door wired shut with baler cord creaked. The unused augers and shoots, the metal braces and unlatched chains seemed to groan. Henry stood and stretched his legs. His back to me, he took a few steps toward the railroad tracks, hitching up his pants with each breathy step.

"Hope you aren't thinking of sticking around here." Henry dipped his head against the breeze and lit another cigarette, puffed it to life. "One time, oh, I guess me and your daddy had been here about five years or so, he brings in this picture of you shooting a layup. I guess you woulda been about eight or nine. He tells me you're gonna play college basketball someday. Said you were his little shooter." Henry took another step toward the tracks, speaking just a tad louder.

"Your daddy's saved my can more than I can count over the years." A sudden burst of coughing overtook him; his body convulsed forward, and he had to spit to get the hacking to stop. I knew his eyes were watery, even with his back to me. From inside the factory, a person yelled, "Oogie, boogie, boogie!" Patsy barked like a police dog, deep and rough, growling. I could hear Larry tell him to sit. Laughter. I turned to look over my shoulder through the dock door. Flashlight beams slashed through the darkness inside, long rays swiping the interior walls, bouncing as their owners ran for cover and a chance to surprise someone. I turned back to listen to Henry, who seemed not to notice the silliness going on in the factory.

"I've sure enjoyed working with you, son," said Henry, his voice hoarse, as if it hurt for him to talk. I was incapable of returning such a kind compliment, too dulled, my brain whitewashed with chemicals. All I could come up with was, "Me too." Henry put his hand out. I took it, and like a preacher in a church, he shook it solidly. "Make your way back over to my side 'fore you leave, will ya? We ain't seen a Moby over there since you left." He made a steely giggle. I stood up, our hands still clasped. He gave me a quick hug and planted a kiss on my cheek. When he turned and walked back toward the dock he called over his shoulder, "Eat your sandwich, son." I watched as his small, dark figure climbed up the dock, black on dark gray, disappearing.

The floppy sandwich dangled from my hand. I raised it, and a piece of the meat fell out, plopped onto the ground. I took a really big bite and chewed it up, swallowed forcefully. Then, in the dark, alone, I threw up Henry's food, a bitter taste in my mouth, as work boots smacked the cement behind me, grown men running in a game of flashlight tag. In just a couple hours the power would be back, and they'd have to work again, but for now, in the darkness, the factory was their joy.

BREAKING IN

Back in Muncie, on the porch of a house that wasn't mine, I thought briefly that what I was doing could be considered breaking and entering. But I convinced myself I hadn't gained entry by guile or force, and I certainly wasn't there to steal or commit an assault. I should have at least been cautious, but a fat joint smoked in the car and chased with several shots of vodka had made me brave.

I fiddled with the key in the lock, twisting it, jimmying the entire handset, the pane in the window rattling and flecks of paint sprinkling the steps. I clutched the white cardboard to my side with my elbow, the poster I would use to complete the class project. The street was quiet and sunny, the shadows of leaves dancing over the new pavement. Grass had grown high in the bumpy yard, and the enormous oak tree was nearly split in two from lightning; the wood seemed to be just parting, opening up, ready to fall apart and expose a whole new creature. The ranch houses on each side were vacant, and for the most part the houses on the rest of the block sat idle as well. Up and down the block, the yards sprung forth with thistle and dead dandelions.

Finally, the old key worked, and I stepped inside. It was boiling hot and musty; the stink of stale beer and dirty carpet clung to the stagnant air. The living room was bare and so were each of the bedrooms. I walked around inside the hollow house and opened some windows. Large hanks of fuzz littered the floors, and loose pen caps, paper clips, and an occasional stray penny stuck to the kitchen's warped linoleum. It was the last house I'd lived in near campus, four blocks away. It had come furnished with only three items: a refrigerator, stove, and kitchen table with the finish peeling off, opaque patches of veneer shedding constantly.

I plopped my book bag on the table and laid the blank cardboard down too, pulled up a metal folding chair from the corner. I'd sat up late many nights at this very table, working on term papers or playing quarters, and it only seemed right to be back to finish up the last class project I'd ever do. In two hours I'd be in class presenting the project, and until just before sunup I hadn't had a clue as to what it would be. It'd come to me as I swept the factory floor, little toes raw inside my boots. I was pushing a broom mindlessly, the power finally back on, all the equipment humming and buzzing, punching holes and sawing edges, dust swarming, the mask over my face so tight it made lines on my cheeks.

I sat down and unzipped the backpack, reached inside and retrieved the papers. At the top of the cardboard I used a ruler to draw two straight lines for the title, lightly, so they'd be easy to erase. The heat was stifling, and sweat began to drip from my nose; I used my T-shirt to dab at it and keep the water from ruining the cardboard. Down near the center I drew smaller lines and numbered them. My hands trembled as I formed the letters, allowing large enough spaces so I could color them in with the black Magic Marker. Before long the title had been drawn. I'd made notes and now dug through the

book bag looking for them. Using them as a guide, I began to print
my observations in pencil:

1) *Many times horseplay is a show of affection.*

2) *Innuendos regarding the buttocks are used to gain intimacy.*

3) *While alcohol use is accepted, drugs are not, and must be
    taken in secret.*

4) *The concept of brotherhood is used to demonstrate a family
    approach to labor.*

5) *Boredom is often the cause of strange behaviors, including pre-
    tending to be a pet, refusing to take safety precautions, and
    obsessing over such things as pop music and hand washing.*

6) *Death is somewhat taboo. There exists a complex and contra-
    dictory approach to handling grief. Crying is seen as weak, and
    most of the time jokes are made pertaining to one's own death.*

7) *Fathers and sons who work together are to act as merely cowork-
    ers; no favoritism is allowed.*

8) *Long hours, double shifts, and overtime are viewed as rites of
    passage.*

9) *A strict hierarchy of classes exists in the workplace. Manage-
    ment sees itself as all-knowing and paternal, while the union
    is dubbed as naïve and without an understanding of business.*

10) *Food, drink, and sharing breaks together serve as the commu-
    nal time to bond. A gifted sandwich or bag of chips can become
    a symbolic sacrifice.*

When I was done I used the black marker to paint in the letters.
One by one I darkened them, blowing on each letter to ensure that
the ink wouldn't smear. A clock on the grimy stove still kept time. I
checked it after every letter, my hand cramping. After the last letter

was filled in, I took a long drink of vodka from the bottle and studied my work—not half bad. I stood and held the cardboard before me, inspecting it like ceiling tile. At the top it read in fat, bold letters: MASCULINITY AND THE WORKPLACE. The ten observations were angled too much, sloping down, but other than that, the project appeared simple and to the point. The only other thing left to do was rehearse the five-minute spiel that was to accompany the project's presentation to the class. With the liquor dulling my hearing, I spoke out loudly. My voice sounded false, as if I'd lost some key inflection that was needed to convey sincerity. I tried again and again. In the empty house, I listened to the echo of my voice as I pretended to perform before the class.

39

HENRY WAS HIS NAME

Fluorescent lights humming, my body leaning toward the announcement under the Plexiglas, I swayed, nearly bowled over. It wasn't a formal card, or even typewritten. The handwriting was curvy and flared. I reread the words and tried to arrange them in my head into something of substance and order. How? I just saw him three days ago. Or had it been longer? I unlatched the plastic door and pulled the pin from the cork, brought the note card out and held it before me, scanning it, turning it over, and finally replacing it back inside the cabinet. Henry was dead.

He told me to come over to his side before I left. He kissed me.

Fog sat thick in the bowl-shaped docking holler. I stood and watched it burble over itself, rise and fall slowly, as if trying to come to life or die. Probably die. Up near a roofline, a single man in his alien suit sucked asbestos fibers into a vacuum strapped to his back. The suction sounded like a faraway plane. I saw Henry's teeth in his pocket, felt the vulnerability of his white bread. I made myself cry.

Walking through the factory would be hell, men stopping me to ask if I'd heard. I would break down, and be shamed, so I opted for a shortcut. I slogged through the back side of the plant, past cob-webbed cubbies and bent steel the color of iodine. As I rounded the corner, the full view of the irrigation ground and the highway beyond flooded my field of vision. The earth steamed. You can spend a thousand hours in a place, think you know every piece of it, and then find a spot where everything looks different and warped, out of sequence and off kilter. In every direction a new tangle of dead grass or upturned hunk of burnt metal showed itself. Sooner or later you've got to leave, and so did material things. It may come as a quick death or a slow corrosion, but everything and everyone went on.

Broad daylight, the starting bell ringing, I staggered over the rocks toward the hidden spot. Only three days ago Henry had stood here, and sat with me. I pulled the cooler from the withered brush, hiding it poorly, the color of the cooler like a hunter's orange vest, easy to spot if anyone was really looking. I flipped the lid open and thrust my hand into the water; four cans of beer swam in murk. I drained each one quickly, the bell ringing for the final time inside. The moment of silence would come right before the fab line forged ahead, cranked out more of something the world really didn't need.

I could hear men in my head saying, "MF's gone. Motherfucker died. Did you hear? Mother's dead."

His name was Henry, and he liked George Jones, peppermint can-dies, and fresh tomatoes—not store bought, but picked right off the vine and eaten like an apple. Henry loved babies and reruns of *The Andy Griffith Show*. Henry smiled better without his teeth than most people do with them. He voted only once in his life, and he didn't like the smell of cabbage cooking. He had jailhouse tattoos that he regretted and a pocket watch he'd found while fishing. Henry was his name, and he worked in the wool mill. He worked every day and always clocked in five minutes before the start of a shift. He bought me a pint of butter pecan ice cream one hot night and surprised me with it, sneaking up from behind and placing the icy container against my neck. "Bet that feels good," he'd said, handing me a flat little wooden spoon.

Henry was his name. He was not just an ex-con, a hillbilly, and a wool mill rat. He was a union brother, a father, and a man that accepted his mistakes. Henry died six months before his retirement, from what management said was lung cancer. He went into the hospital complaining of difficulty breathing and was dead three days later.

One of the diseases associated with asbestosis is lung cancer, made more probable by smoking. In fact, workers who are exposed to asbestos and who smoke are ninety times more likely to contract lung cancer than workers who are free of either of these deadly hazards.

Henry was his name, and he worked at the factory for nearly forty years.

40

CRY BABY

To my astonishment, my father asked me to attend Henry's funeral. He knew I was friends with him, and perhaps it was a safe way for him to relay that he was scared too, needed some company at the viewing. All summer he'd kept me at a distance when it came to his union brothers and their hurt, but in the steel house, him in his underwear, me in a pair of sweats, he said, "You wanna come to the services?" He slurred the words and looked as if he had a fever, cheeks blushed, and the spot between his eyebrows wet. I accepted his invitation and got up to get dressed.

The funeral home was across the road from an egg-processing plant, where workers held the eggs up to bright lights to check for embryos. The acrid sulfur stench drifted over the highway and hung above the steaming pavement where my dad parked the car. The egg factory, Celotex, and a few other rusty, smokestacked factories were the only significant employers in town.

My dad wore a short-sleeved shirt tucked into a pair of gray pleated pants, a shiny black belt strapped around his ample waist.

I had on a suit I'd bought on sale at JC Penney, a meager addition to my interview wardrobe. I'd also purchased a cheap briefcase, a perfect-bound dictionary, and a pen-and-pencil set that gleamed with silver, all in hopes that I'd actually find a job with a bachelor's degree in psychology.

Our car didn't have air conditioning, and by the time we reached the funeral home I could see a large dark spot on my father's back and feel the sweat dripping off my nose. I imagined we were leaving a trail of water droplets behind that we could follow back to the car.

As it turned out, Henry had been diagnosed a couple months earlier with lung cancer and kept it to himself. Some said Henry may have never known what the doctor had really said, that perhaps the terms the physician used didn't make sense to him, but I don't believe that. Too many men had died before him for Henry to have not known he was working on borrowed time.

As my dad signed the guest book at the little podium, I spotted a group of guys from the factory standing in a circle, shirts damp, hands shoved in pants pockets, somber but fiery-eyed from shots of schnapps in the parking lot. They nodded at us, and in unison my father and I returned the gesture.

As my dad marched us toward the front of the funeral home to stare down at Henry in his casket, I longed for a bottle. Cold air from a large vent above us hit my damp back and gave me the chills. I felt utterly out of place in my interview suit. Henry's family had dressed him in a blue work shirt, buttoned to his chin, no tie. His thick hair, brushed back, shone under the lights. He didn't look "eaten up" with cancer, like some of the factory guys had said during lunch breaks. Instead he looked as if he were napping during downtime, when the line would jam and we'd all get to grab a few winks before it roared back to life.

Ever since I was a kid, I've cried freely and without much provocation: when baby pigs died on the farm, when a kid at school would sock me in the shoulder, when my first girlfriend dumped me. I embraced crying; it made me feel better, released some grim, throttling tension in my stomach. But my dad hated it. I'd never seen him cry, not once, not even a misty tearing-up. His parents had died, his dreams had been shattered, and his friends were dying, and yet he always acted the stable man, capable of fixing any problem, coolheaded and unemotional, while I did everything to stifle my tears, including a lip-puckering technique that made me appear more crotchety than sad. Right then, next to Henry's simple wooden casket, I wanted more than anything for my dad to break down, to fill his shirt pockets with tears. But, of course, he didn't. He only bowed in the direction of Henry's widow, handed Henry's son a check in an envelope, then turned to walk back up the aisle toward the exit. I stumbled behind him, wiping my tears on my suit jacket sleeves.

In the parking lot the sun made everything silver and painfully bright, the air so thick and humid it felt like some roving, mad wall of red-hot anger. I intentionally lagged behind my father as I tried to swallow the king-sized lump in my throat. I stopped and watched the different groups of men standing in little circles, talk of asbestos and poisoning drifting over the flat black inferno, intermingled with calm chitchat regarding overtime pay and the new kind of gloves the supply room had recently ordered. My dad was standing by the car, beckoning me with his hairy forearm to get a move on; from that distance, he was a blurry figure, a heat-wave mirage. As I walked away, I heard one of the men with sallow eyes spit a ball of phlegm onto the sizzling ground, the sound of someone's dress shoe tapping the pavement as he tried to put out a cigarette. For the first time, I really listened; the coughing and hacking of the men sounded like a sickly herd of wild horses, semi-free but thinning, visibly strong but deceptive, their canters growing weak, and water nowhere to be found.

41

BUSTED

"Get her up," my dad said, his voice crackling. My mother wouldn't have it though, and rolled from one side of the bed to the other, a horizontal Bugs Bunny on the run. In their small bedroom, she cried and kicked. I scooted along the wall and the side of the bed, but she rolled in the other direction and kept doing so every time we thought we had her. The fur on the Bugs costume, in contact with her frilly bedspread, produced a great amount of static, and my mother's hair lifted from the sides and made her look like a Kewpie doll. She picked up the pace of her rolling, flopping back and forth, each time my dad and I missing her by a fraction of an inch. Finally, my dad grabbed hold of her by the Bugs butt, the material there saggy and plentiful, and yanked her into a sitting position.

"Doris," he said, "you've got to go with the police. The store pressed charges. You've got to go. We'll follow you in the car." My mother sobbed and began tearing at her costume. "I didn't mean to take them. It was an accident," she bawled.

Outside in our driveway a police car sat waiting on us. The call had come while we were at work. My mother had been caught shoplifting a pair of earrings. The cops had told us that the store manager had twenty-four hours to make up his mind, and he did. Now, she would have to be booked and charged.

The sirens outside flashed red, bouncing off the steel house, sneaking into the windows, as my father calmed her down. Suddenly, my mother stopped crying and stood up. She stepped out of the costume and brushed off the front of her Arby's uniform. "Let your mother fix her hair and then she'll go," she said, addressing me, ignoring my father.

She left the bedroom and slid into the bathroom, the sound of Aqua Net spraying just seconds later. My father and I sat on the bed. I couldn't distinguish the smell of his liquory breath from my own. He rubbed his hands together, and it sounded like he might be sanding a board.

"I don't know what I'm gonna do with that woman," he said, hanging his head just a bit.

"Which one?" I asked, nervous, but not caring.

He popped his head up and looked me in the eye. I stared at him. On the dresser was a black and white photo of my parents in high school, thirty years earlier, him in a posed free throw and her at the top of a pyramid of smiling cheerleaders. My dad stood up, brushed past me, and went out, heading for the front door. He said behind him, "Make sure she brings her wallet—they're gonna want to see her ID."

With my mother still in the bathroom, I snuck to the window to see what he was doing. In the driveway he smoked a cigarette with the cops, offering to light theirs from his matches. Before they'd finish the Salems, he'd broker a deal, ask that he be allowed to bring her in the next day. But I wouldn't know that until later. Now, as I watched my father with the cops, my mother nearly scared the puke out of me. She'd also snuck up quietly to the window. Her hair was stacked in an outrageous pile, high and glued à la Tammy Wynette. She looked out the window and sighed.

"He's all your mother's ever wanted. We've dated since eighth grade. Your mother loves him. And I know he loves her."

One of the cops laughed at something my father said as he turned toward the cruiser. The deputy ducked inside and shut off the sirens, and the driveway was dark again. I moved toward my mother and patted her on the arm. She sobbed and I held her. The tumbleweed on her head scratched my nose. She said, "Your mother thinks his hairpiece makes him look just like he did senior year." Clearly, she was intoxicated from the Aqua Net. I didn't say anything. I could feel her tears and snot soaking through my shirt as she whispered in my ear, "Could you spare twenty bucks?"

SIPHON SON

RVs rolled into the parking lot with purpose. The men behind the wheels performed exact turns, their arms stiff and poised as they glided into the vacant parking spots near the office usually reserved for the big shots in from company headquarters in Tampa. While the asbestos removers had vanished, their jobs supposedly finished, a second round of personnel had arrived to demonstrate the company's concern. The RVs housed medical equipment. If a worker wished, he could undergo a battery of tests to determine if he needed a referral to a lung specialist. Slogans such as "Prevention, Responsibility, and Accuracy" covered the sides of the RVs.

The doors opened up and a crew of technicians poured out and filed down the sidewalk toward the office entrance. I watched along with several other men on break, cigarettes pluming smoke around their heads, as the shade inside the office conference room was slowly lowered. The workers turned their heads back to the RVs. A man said, "One of them would make a nice home, wouldn't it?" The others agreed, eyes squinted against the sting of their smoke, nodding. "You could just about keep a whole family in there."

One by one the men finished their cigarettes, flipping the butts onto the same sidewalk I'd just swept. They followed one another into the door of the factory, the last man stopping briefly to survey the scene again, flashing a quick, trenchant smile in my direction. The RVs were worth more than their combined pensions, and the smile was meant to convey astonishment.

The bristles on the sidewalk scratched lines into the thick dust as I pushed the heavy broom forward, making a heap of dirt near the bin. Several carloads of men returning from their break flew inside the gates as they tried to beat the clock. Up the steps they raced, not noticing the RVs or me cleaning up. The last car in the gate coasted and didn't even sound like the engine was running; it was my dad's. He rolled into a parking spot away from the main part of the factory, near the loading docks. He stepped out of the car and mashed out his cigarette, then tucked the butt into his jean cuff. For a moment, he peered over at the RVs, then shook his head, as if saying, "No, thank you." He tried to walk a straight line toward the small set of steps that led up to his warehouse office, but he slanted off course and had to right himself, aim again. He staggered up the steps and went inside, the door slapping behind him.

Before long, after I'd scooped up pan after pan of dust, butts, and vending machine wrappers, the men from the RVs exited the front office, organized and quiet. They split up and climbed back inside the giant vehicles, each roaring to life again, backing up to cross the parking lot. The drivers pulled the RVs into a patch of tan grass next to a water hookup, then cut the motors once more. They'd begin their testing at the end of the shift.

I pushed my broom under some benches, drawing it back like a net, capturing even more trash. These were the same benches I'd been held at as a kid, the same ones where I'd nibbled a proffered Nutty Bar or Hostess Fruit Pie. Henry and Jerry and Mr. Raines had sat on the benches, eaten their snacks and lunches along with a hundred others. I took a seat myself now and pulled the program for the graduation ceremony from my pocket. By the same time the next day, I'd be a college graduate, the first in my family. The leaflet was printed with fancy cursive lettering and spelled out which dean would say what and at what time. Some music would be performed, and a reading or two would occur. All told, it would take less than an hour.

I was staring at the paper when the office door opened up. I rose quickly to my feet and began working under the tables again. A man in a necktie looked in my direction and nodded. The broom caught on something substantial under the last section of benches. Pulling the entire mound toward me, I waited until the man got in his car and left the parking lot. Then I bent down and flipped the hard clods off my find, dusting off a half-drunk bottle of gin.

Once, when I was ten years old, while my brothers and dad burned brush in a river bottom field, I took two packs of my dad's Salems and stuffed them down a groundhog hole. I'd recently learned about the hazards of smoking and wanted my father not to die. When he walked to the truck for a break, he noticed his recently purchased cigarettes were gone and quizzed us all. I broke down and confessed within three minutes. He had me show him where the groundhog den was, and he easily reached into the lip of the hole, roots dangling from where loose earth peppered the leaves below, and retrieved his smokes. He gave me a lecture on hard work and the value of the almighty dollar before going back to the field, a Salem dangling from his lips and a little grin on his face. I took his smile to mean he was happy I'd tried to protect him.

Just in case I was being tested, on the outside chance my old man wanted me to stop him, I took the bottle of gin and stuffed it inside my waistband. I'd siphon it off, so he wouldn't have to do it himself.

THE GRADUATE

L ooking out into the crowd all I could see was darkness, no eyeglasses reflecting light, not a single face illuminated with pride, nothing. It was as if I were about to receive my fake diploma in the abyss of some pitch-black tanker. The assistant dean handed me the blank paper with a brief, contrived smile and a handshake. I patted the railing along the steps and felt my way down to the third row of metal chairs. With a last name starting with C, I would have a lot of people to wait on before I could shuffle out of the auditorium into the bright daylight. It'd been a summer of funerals, and now, sitting in the dark, watching others climb the stage to receive their futures, I couldn't help but feel it was meaningless.

By the timid light of the tiny bulbs lining the aisle I found the flask at my feet and bent to take a swig, then sat back up in the hard chair and looked around. My parents were in attendance, out there somewhere in the dark, but I wouldn't see them afterward; they both had to leave for work as soon as I left the stage with my bogus diploma. I hadn't told Derrick and Darren I'd be going through the ceremonies, knowing they'd certainly take time out of their busy work schedules to be there, and I didn't want them wasting time on an empty ceremony.

People were becoming restless as the last group to receive their diplomas filed onto the stage. The loved ones in attendance had always envisioned their babies graduating outside in the spring, trees in blossom, pink petals covering their black gowns, not inside a refrigerated theater in August. But it was so freaking hot at the summer-term graduation that grandma and grandpa would've passed out had it been held outside.

After the ceremony, out on the green lawn, I stood and observed the people milling around. To my surprise there were happy faces, gleeful and proud parents and elderly relations, all floating around one another, talking incessantly about the heat, the drought, the difference between inside and out. I spotted a couple students I'd known, but made no attempt to move. I wanted to; I wished my body would go one way or another, make a decision. Instead, my feet remained planted as I noticed how most students were wearing casual dress clothes under their gowns, and I sported the JC Penney suit I'd worn to Henry's funeral. I couldn't have looked more foolish if I'd donned a baby blue tuxedo.

The chatter about plans roved around me. "Oh, a master's in special ed, that would be nice." "What's that? You're going overseas to work in the Peace Corps? How wonderful!" "Don't tell me, Suzie, you're going to spend another hunk of your daddy's money on a trip around the world to find yourself before you settle down to work for him in his office? My goodness!"

Finally I began to move. I plowed my way through the crowd and toward the sidewalk, pushing past pretty-in-pinks and dashing-in-button-downs, their faces looking as if I might be a walking cow pie. I had to be back to the factory to pull a sixteener in just a couple hours, so I headed home to the steel house to keep secrets and not sleep. As I stepped down the hill I looked over my shoulder at the masses gathered across the verdant turf. They looked causal and at ease, while I felt out of place and lost. Tipsy, I pondered the possibility that I might be able to start a new life. Then, I tripped and fell, and in my insightful musing busted my ass.

DOG ON COUCH

Three days after graduation and I was working the tile-load-out job again, glue caked to my long sleeves and smatters of it drying on my boots as I tried to finish a double shift. My legs trembled with weakness, the kneecaps popping as I stooped to pick up another box of tile. Mind churning, I made myself focus on the task, but it was no good. The same thought reeled through my brain. *Lifer? Lifer? Will you be? Should you? Why are you still here? Hit the road. Why don't you take off and leave this behind? Dumb fuck. You've got a degree at least, go, flee, scoot, amscray!*

I struggled with a box and it fell, denting a corner, possibly damaging the beveled edges on the tile. I heaved it from the floor and hunch-backed it to a skid, marked down my mistake and pinned the carbon copy duplicate to the damaged box with a pushpin. Suddenly the line stopped, not unusual, but a bell rang too, indicating something else had happened that would take more than a few minutes to fix.

High, I pulled the remaining boxes from the line with intense speed and determination, anxious to get them out of the way so I could go out back to the tracks for more. Jerking the glue gun free of its gummy metal holster, I shot globular pellets over the last tier of boxes and placed a cardboard tie on top of the chunky glue. I used the foot pedal to raise the pallet up to the proper height, done until the line would start again.

Since the ceremonies, I'd worked hard at making myself eat, trying to force down whatever I could, cereal, candy bars, a shake, or tasteless vending machine sandwich. I thought of the 3 Musketeers bar I had in the cooler near the tracks. More memos had appeared stressing that management was serious about enforcing the long-standing policies on alcohol use on the job. With the men in the RVs testing workers and reporting their findings inside the front office, everything was to look official and proper.

How long can a man occupy the same space, the same never-changing routine, before going mad? For some, endlessly returning to the same place and things offers order and security, while for others, it's a daily death. Most find internal methods to change that space, even if it's only by perception. I looked around the worn-down earth where the cooler was hidden, all the same rusty objects in their place, the sun setting—even the birds seemed like all the others before. And the temperature didn't move up or down enough to make a difference. The summer had gone on for years, each day a perfect match to the ones before, hot and dull and without end.

A wad of fluffy candy bar in my mouth, I popped a can of beer and slurped the suds. Without any notice a dog appeared at my shins, pushed its head against the sticky glue on my pants, his nose now holding a smudge of the white, as I reached down, removed his cap, and petted his greasy hair. Patsy rolled onto his side and allowed me access to his grimy gut, mustard stains and crusty sauces splashed across the bib of the overalls.

"I put you in the class project, boy," I said, continuing to rub behind his ears. "The prof thought you might suffer from goal denial.

What do you think, fella, huh? Oh, that's a good boy. I got an A."
Patsy panted and leapt back on all fours, began licking at my hands,
as I moved them as quickly as chopping blades, trying to keep his
tongue from making contact. If there'd been a ball I would've played
fetch with him.

The sun slipped down the sky, giving the horizon a golden hue,
streaks of blue and pink cracking the entire view, as if something was
about to burst. Tiny droplets of rain fell from above, only a sprinkle,
but more than we'd had in weeks. Patsy took delight in the moisture
and pretended to be chasing his tail.

"Listen, boy, I'm going to ask you some questions, and you bark
once for no and twice for yes, OK?" Patsy yapped two times. The
professor had told me about using heuristic techniques with Patsy,
communicating to him in his own language, leading Old Yeller to his
own answers.

With the sprinkle petering off, I asked, "Did your parents let you
have a dog?"

"Woof, woof."

"What happened to him, did he die?" Two more barks.

"Did he die naturally or from an accident? One for the first, two
if it's the second."

"Ruff, ruff!" Patsy played the obedient Lab before a roaring fire-
place; his posture was regal and proud.

"Good boy. Now, when was the accident, when you were a pup or
full-grown dog? One bark for pup, two for full grown."

"Ruff," barked Patsy, solemn.

"I'm sorry, boy. That's never easy to lose someone or something
you love so young."

Patsy remained two feet in front of me, the little pitter of rain
now gone, the sky darkening. A train came into view and the first
few cars passed us. I was about to ask him some more questions
when an awful screeching sound, metal on metal, hot and panicky,

pierced the humid air. The train before us was locking up, applying all its force to try and stop, the cars slowing down with every millisecond, flashing graffiti, the sense of something awful building in the opposite direction.

45

UNHOLY UNION

A statue of Mary, one of Jesus, and a few nameless saints appeared to me, all of them whirling around the rooftop of the church, peeking from the sides of the bell, their hands bigger than normal, extra large and reaching out. In the scorching, dark heat, cold air rushed over my skin, as if in a frozen barn lot of my youth, all the stock bawling for the two-inch-thick ice to be broken, setting free the frigid water, giving them life. *You pound your fist into it, bust it open, drag out the fat, slippery chunks of ice, toss them over the fence. Hit the hard surface like it's the face of a bully. Punch through it fast, and it won't hurt but an instant; your knuckles will get relief as soon as they plunge into the twenty-below-zero tank.*

Sitting on the church steps, the vision of the tundra vanished and I wondered why it'd come at all. Shivering in droughtlike conditions can only be explained by the presence of something cold inside. I hadn't known the little girl, but I'd seen her in town, outside this very church, coasting on her bike, little knees scabbed, shiny hair lifting up as she gained speed, feet deliberately off the spinning pedals, a

233

gap-toothed grin pushing her cheeks up. She was simply a little kid on a bike, her whole, not-yet-flawed life before her. A deep shudder quaked my stomach, and I threw up in some bushes, beer and whiskey gutting my nostrils as it foamed out of them.

I replayed in my mind the events before getting drunk in the tavern and stumbling toward the pulsating church. How the train had finally ground to a stop, how quiet it seemed then; even the factory's noise was drowned out by the silence. Nothing could compete with the quiet. The screeching train and then the quiet; these images were etched inside me, along with a recurring thought. *Carl.* He was forbidden.

I hadn't been able to stand around with the others and trade the snippets of rumor that ran rampant after the sheriffs had walked into the factory, their brown uniforms and gleaming badges so out of place in our dusty, itchy hellhole. I'd been sitting alone in a lunchroom not many men used; they ate either outside at the benches or in the break area. When Carl came he was so quiet I didn't even hear him. One instant I was alone and the next he was across the table from me, pouring steaming coffee into his silver cup, tiny hands, rough like my dad's, trying their best not to shake. His presence had made me start with the shivering.

I'd not sought him out, hadn't approached him on my own; it was a coincidence that we'd both chosen to hide out in the same unfrequented room. Carl had kept his head down, but felt my stare and looked up. His eyes were full of thick tears, glassy and brown, an expression of begging at the borders, where the whites were laced with red. I'd hardly gotten the words, "I'm sorry," out before I broke down. Carl reached over and patted my hands and then hung his head again. I felt ashamed that all I could give him was more burden and pushed my chair back, got up and went to the door. The image of Carl's back was pitiful, hunched over, the nape of his neck sunburned, the graying hair at the base gently curled.

As I'd stepped outside I'd heard a moan from the lunchroom, a kind of steady grunt that ended abruptly. And that's what made me simply leave the factory, walk toward the tavern in town, the booze finally depositing me on the steps of the church.

The little girl had tried to ride her bike through the railroad crossing but didn't make it. Men in the factory said the best things they knew how, just like with Carl's daughter's death. "She went quick, we can thank God for that." Or, "She wouldn't have known what hit her." These things were said to be comforting, and to comfort themselves, but after a while, after friends and children die for no good reason, the statements begin to carry an angry pitch, each word spit out like a hot pellet, something seething underneath, an intolerance for any more of it.

Now, as I snuck around the back of the church, I knew it was all over, that I'd had enough and couldn't stay on. Scared or not, I'd have to leave the factory.

I tried the rear door of the church, but it was locked with a dead-bolt. A spigot dripped water nearby, the rhythmic *drop, drop, drop* like a chant. I sat down again on the steps of the church and really tried to pray. Nothing would come. Every time I started I couldn't find the words to ask for mercy on the families. Each prayer started out with a sweeping, grandiose benediction and then fizzled out. Since the Incredible Hulk had saved me at the church in junior high, I'd kept up with my prayers, said roughly the same thing each night as I lay in bed, drifting in and out of consciousness. But now all that would come to me were some rambling, dislocated words. In Sunday school the Hulk had talked about paradise, called it "the abode of God." The phrase clanged around in my head and I became angry. A car thumped over a pothole as I wiped snot off my face with the back of my hand, stood up.

Headlights poured over me and I squinted into the glare. I couldn't see and thought for sure the police had been called, taken away from their solemn duties at the railroad tracks. The lights went off and a voice called to me. "Come on." I could see the orange nip of a cigarette dangling from the driver's mouth, smell his cologne. "We're taking Carl home," my dad said, his voice milder, apologetic. I got in the front seat with them, Carl between me and my dad. In the humid dark of the night, my dad put the car in gear. "How about we go have some coffee and a fritter?" Carl nodded in agreement as my dad backed away from the church. The weak light from the dashboard shone on our fronts. I almost broke down again when my dad reached for his friend's hand and patted softly, so fast and efficient and merciful. I believed the movement was my answered prayer.

46

YOUR MOTHER'S YELLOW SON

Derrick's car was all cleaned out, vacuumed, wiped down with Armor-All, washed, and waxed. In the pocket of my jeans, the bus ticket was tucked away like a winning lottery ticket. I drove on autopilot. My dad and I were due at work in a few hours, but I knew I'd never go.

I pulled off at nearly the same spot where I'd spied on my dad knocking at Jerry's door. The trailer seemed to hover in the distance, heat shimmering off the metal. I stepped out of the car, clutching the journal Jerry had bought me a subscription to. My boots dragged through the brittle grass in the ditch, stirring up something that filled my eyes with tears, my nose with water. Halfway up the road I stopped. A jet's white contrail widened in the sky, a cottony scar dropping off behind a hilly nest of trees. I should have kept walking, but didn't. Instead I turned sharply on my heels and picked up the pace back to the car. I told myself I'd call him later, when I got settled in, figured out what to do next.

Back in the car, the coconut air freshener in the shape of a tropi-
cal tree smelled too sweet. Derrick would hate it. I pulled it off the
rearview mirror and turned the ignition. I performed the same three-
point turn as last time, ignoring Jerry's delicate tin house getting farther and farther away over my shoulder.

I left a note scrawled in pencil on the dash, then hid the keys under
the mat on the duplex's porch. When my brother arrived home he'd
have his vehicle back. Completing his generous act gave me pleasure, although I'd done nothing to deserve it. I climbed down the
steps and started on foot toward my parents' house, a good twenty
minutes away.

I stalked my father as he slept. His full cheeks glowed as if rouged
while he twitched and snorted. I crept around the room, leaning
toward his bed, inspecting his body. I wanted to see if I could detect
in him any signs of the killer that was taking the lives of the members
of Local 563. I tracked his scent—the Stetson cologne and mouth-
wash—skulking along the perimeter of the bed, the sunlight peeking
through the curtains and falling at his feet. He mumbled something
and rolled over, and for a brief moment I thought I'd heard him say
he was sorry. I stood stone-still and listened again, but the only sound
was his scratchy breathing.

I paced the shag carpet and watched him as if he were an ill child.
I felt my stomach twist with worry. All summer long, I'd thought I
was watching my father for signs of cancer—and I was—but I was
also trying to find in him traces of guilt or love or at least fear. We
were both scared, me with the notion I might not ever realize my
dreams, and him frightened that he'd never get another chance to
realize his. For a moment, I thought of waking him and attempting
a tearful farewell, but in the end, I just watched him. I walked to the
door and turned back to give him one last opportunity to confess in
his sleep. He curled up soundlessly, all of a sudden breathing like an
angel. As much as I'd wanted to harm him, all I felt as I watched my

dad was an achy, deep love. I left him there in that steel house, protected from everything except what would hurt the most, what could
inflict the most damage—himself.

I got a lift into town from a fellow college kid, who dropped me
off in front of Arby's. I didn't know where to put my suitcase, which
held my interview suit, my dictionary, and my briefcase. I settled
on tucking it beside the trash can outside, then proceeded inside. I
wanted to tell my mother I was leaving, but somehow I believed she
already knew. The restaurant air smelled like warm bread, not the
greasy fries I'd expected. My mother stood behind the counter in her
dark blue and tan uniform and silly bow tie. She waved, and a smile
creased her face, then disappeared as she beckoned me over. Something thickened in the back of my mouth, and I felt feverish.

My mother tapped her wristwatch as if she'd been expecting me,
and said, "Your mother's break is right now." As we walked down
a sticky hallway to a drab break room filled with round tables and
even stickier chairs, I thought about her cartoon-character costumes
and it broke my heart, a loyal employee working her ass off for nothing more than a lousy assistant manager's paycheck. The corporate
world of fast food didn't deserve her. The Looney Tunes promotion
had been put to rest, replaced by some sports theme. I imagined her
donning a homemade Colts uniform with a frilly mane and askew ass
tail, her day crew shuddering in their teenage shoes.

We sat down at a table, and I was unable to look her in the eye. It
was as if metal rods immobilized my neck. I'd been a coward all summer, and now, when I'd planned to be strong for her, all that would
come out of me were snotty, gasping sobs. My mother got up from
her chair and came around to me. I stood, and we hugged tightly, the
smell of her hairspray thick in my face as I stooped to hold her; she
seemed smaller than ever. She held me until I regained control over
myself, and then I kissed her forehead.

"My suitcase is outside," I said.

"You'd better get going, then," she said in a tremulous voice. "Your mother's got to get back, too." She hugged me again and whispered in my ear, "Be careful, baby. Write your mother with your pretty words."

I walked out the door and back down the hallway, the soles of my shoes sticking to the grimy linoleum. I had no idea what I would do once I got to Indianapolis, or what kind of job would be available to me, but I had to get away, abandon what I both loved and despised. Maybe only the kids of parents who never went to college, who didn't get their chance for the life they dreamed of would understand, but if I could use one word to describe what I was doing, it would be betrayal. Once you leave your family and go another way, there's no turning back, even if you feel damned forever for doing it.

EPILOGUE

Just a few days before Christmas, after I'd been working as a human resources clerk in Indianapolis for almost two months, I got a call from the pastor of my junior-high church. He told me my father had been caught sitting in a dump truck outside the factory, still on the clock, a six-pack of beer on the cold seat. To keep his job, my father had to attend a thirty-day substance-abuse program at the county hospital. He had asked for me to come home, the pastor said.

My father and I hadn't spoken since I left that day on a Greyhound bus, and I wasn't certain why he would want me to come see him now, under these circumstances. My mother asked me to come, too. She said on the phone, "Come if you can. It might help you both."

So I drove the two hours north and parked in the visitors' lot behind the hospital. It was ten degrees outside, and the forecast was for eleven inches of snow by suppertime. I waited for a counselor to emerge from his cubicle office, then spent several minutes talking with him about the finer points of my father's "addiction."

I had trouble with the term, but didn't say so. It made me uneasy, encroached on territory I hadn't yet ceded.

"He's a complex man, your dad," the counselor said to me, his thin mustache twitching. "Been drinking heavily in secret for years." He paused briefly before going on. "His substance addictions are persistent, and they're substantial." Then he returned to his office to confer with my dad. The snow was already beginning to fall when the counselor came back. "I forgot to tell you," he said. "Right now, he may only have visitors in peer group." He motioned for me to follow him through the security door.

Inside the cold cinder-block room, chairs were set up in a circle. I sat down, not knowing what to expect. A dozen or so other family members of those sentenced to treatment sat haphazardly around the room. My mother couldn't come; she had been promoted and was in mandatory supervisor training. I had little time to think about her absence, however, as another door opened in the back of the room and a line of men and women wearing robes and pajamas filed in. My father was in the middle of the line and looked completely out of place without his usual factory clothes. His bald head, no longer covered by the toupee, looked exposed and vulnerable. He took his seat and smiled gently at me as he adjusted his pale blue robe. On his feet he wore tube socks and a pair of black slippers. The look on his face was one I'd never seen on him before; he was resigned. Before us, on an ocher wall, an enormous chart of the twelve steps hung like the Commandments.

"Who'd like to start?" asked a counselor.

My father's hand shot up. "That'd be me," he said confidently. He got up from his chair, dragged it to the center of the circle, sat down not ten feet from me, and said, "My name's Dan Crandell, and I'm an alcoholic."

In unison, the crowd said blandly, "Welcome, Dan."

He wasted no time. "My son's here," he began, "and I want to apologize to him." His hands shook as he removed his glasses to wipe tears from his eyes. At that moment, I hated him more than ever. I hated him for having made me worry that he'd die all summer long; I hated him for finally letting me see him cry; and I hated him for starting down the long road toward becoming a better man, while I couldn't budge. Even with my new office job I was still using—out of the factory, but still living by its habits. I wanted to run, jump out the window.

"Doug, we need you to tell us how you feel," the counselor pled. My father sat still in his chair, his face accepting, willing to take whatever I would heave at him.

"I'm not going to talk to my dad in front of all these people." My vision blurred, tears hot and thick. I felt the group's eyes on me, their silence urging me forward, trying to help me. I stammered and choked up. My dad said in a kind voice, "Take your time, son." When I was able to speak, I was shocked at how easily I told him exactly how I felt.

I must have said I hated him a hundred times before it was over. For the first time in my life, I didn't have to sputter through dammed-up emotion, or choke down tears. In a room filled with complete strangers, I let my father have it.

When it was over, I got to sit with him for five minutes. "You did a good job, son," he said. "I deserved that." Then he laughed and said, "But don't feel bad; yours was nothing compared to what your mother said."

That night I stayed with my mother while the snow piled up outside and my dad slept in a hospital bed less than a mile away, locked away with the truth and his newfound tears.

AFTERWORD

Fifteen years after I worked the summer at the factory, I am home for my parents' forty-eighth wedding anniversary. It's cold out but my father meets me on the street. I notice brand-new side-walks stretching the length of his property and leading right up to the front and back steps of a nice house they were finally able to buy.

"Did the city put those in?"

He stops and admires the work. "Nope, they pay for the materials, but you have to arrange for the labor." He's smiling now, raking his foot along the surface. The concrete is nearly white and at least six inches thick, the edges smooth and exact. The neighbors' sidewalks are new too, but theirs are thin and uneven.

"Must've cost quite a bit. Did you hire a professional?"

He laughs and pushes his hat back on his head, the afternoon light full on his smooth face. These days, he's a changed man, talkative and more open. He's become a grandfather of six, and they all love him. He plays games and reads books with them, and makes their favorite meals.

"If you call Carl and me professionals. I promised him a good supper and all the cups of coffee he could drink."

He's fully smiling. I'm speechless as I think about the two of them still working together, their knees bad from thirty years in the factory, and yet the product of their labor so fine and exact. I long to know what they talked about while making the sidewalk together, as they took breaks and sipped coffee. Their lifelong friendship is something I envy. Carl is the one that knows my father best; he's been ministered to by my dad, cared for, and they have a mutual bond. I stare along with dad at the sidewalk, the two of us quiet as the wind picks up. I think of the basketball court and the concrete they laid for me years ago. I can see my dad and Carl working in the factory, in an open field, inside the city limits, and in a hundred other ways, the task their medicine.

"He's always been good at concrete work. Could've done that for a living instead." He doesn't finish the thought, but we both know he means instead of Celotex.

I watch him as he looks off into the distance, his eyes older, and puffier underneath, but clear. We've left our addictions behind, something that took me longer to accomplish than him. For years after working at the factory I used drugs and alcohol off and on, hiding it, until my child was born, and I finally found something bigger than myself to fill the void.

. . .

In 2001, the Celotex plant in Lagro, Indiana, was significantly downsized. The union my father and I belonged to is nearly gone. The factory that once employed over one hundred people now operates on a skeleton crew—all that's left is the wool mill. The bales of rock wool are still shipped out, but business has dwindled to a trickle. The factory no longer makes ceiling tile; those jobs have all gone overseas. The rest of the plant has either been bulldozed over or boarded up. By the time the manufacturing line was shut down and my dad was forced to take early retirement, he had worked at Celotex for nearly three decades. His union job allowed him to raise five kids, pay the bills, and help put me through college. Surely Celotex was not a perfect place, and it would be sentimental to lament its closing without also focusing on the problems, but in the end, the factory was to both of us, and to our union brothers, both a blessing and a curse. Some men received the paltry settlements that the company offered, but most opted to just keep working until it was downsized.

The difficult task of discerning the cause of asbestosis poisoning has left the issue of who's to blame for the deaths at Celotex mired in confusion. Because cigarette smoking greatly increases the chance of lung cancer developing in a person exposed to workplace asbestos, it has made class-action lawsuits against companies very difficult to pursue.

Less than two years after I left the factory, my friend Jerry died, too. All the deaths at the factory should be remembered, and more importantly the lives of these men, but it's been Jerry's passing that's taught me so much. For years I'd think I'd heard his voice or saw him in a crowd. At railroad crossings, where tall corn warmed in the sun, I'd swear I saw him slip from the deep green and onto the tracks, beckoning me to follow. And once, I even believed his ghost had come to me at the foot of my bed. Now, though, it's his friendship I remember most, and that can be a source of pain and joy, but mostly joy.

. . .

My brothers and sisters and I have gotten our parents a big sheet cake from Kroger, with pearly icing and a horde of candles, forty-eight of them. We sit around the dinner table, grandkids too, and

I am taken aback to see my parents holding hands. They've found a way to forgive each other, accept each other's flaws. Before long, the evening is almost over. My father stands, and I realize he's going to make a toast. He holds a glass of sweet tea in his meaty hand and looks down at my mother, then at the rest of us. He says, "Thank you all for coming." Dad chokes up a little, and then manages, "I love you."

And just like that, I've learned something else from him. There's no reason to be ashamed of your past, if you're willing to change. To be a real man, you have to submit to being forgiven, and you have to be strong enough to forgive others. Of course, he hasn't said this, but I feel it when he sits back down and nods his head at me from across the table, winks. When I leave, he hugs me so hard I think I'll break.

ACKNOWLEDGMENTS

I'm grateful to my family for allowing me to write about our lives. I enjoy more love from them than I deserve. I am especially indebted to my father, who has shown great patience with my writing. I love him very much.

For their early assistance, I would like to thank Chris Weidler, Kris Hunt, Mo Bunnell, Craig Haecker, Steve Hall, Cary Griffin, Jeff Curtis, and Darren and Derrick Crandell, all good men who helped give me the courage and direction I needed for this book. May they be thoroughly blessed.

Without the financial help of the Goldfarb Fellowship at the Virginia Center for the Creative Arts, I never would have been able to make it through. Also, a huge thanks goes to Andrew Snee and Sy Syfransky at *The Sun* magazine, where several pieces of this book first appeared.

At Chicago Review Press I am deeply thankful for the helpful editing of Cynthia Sherry and Lisa Reardon, and for the support and aid of Gerilee Hundt, Brooke Kush, Lisa Rosenthal, Allison Felus, and Jon Hahn.

I am grateful for the love of Kennedy, my daughter, who has given me so much laughter, compassion, and joy that I sometimes wonder when I'll awake from the dream. Also, my gratitude goes out to Nancy Brooks-Lane and Walker Lane for their support, help, and affection.

Lastly, I will forever be connected to all the union members, past and present, of the Local 563 Paper Workers Union.